William H. Vibbert

A Guide to Reading the Hebrew Text

For the use of beginners

William H. Vibbert

A Guide to Reading the Hebrew Text
For the use of beginners

ISBN/EAN: 9783337316167

Printed in Europe, USA, Canada, Australia, Japan

Cover: Foto ©Paul-Georg Meister /pixelio.de

More available books at **www.hansebooks.com**

A

GUIDE

TO

READING THE HEBREW TEXT;

FOR THE

USE OF BEGINNERS.

BY THE

REV. W. H. VIBBERT, M.A.,

PROFESSOR OF HEBREW IN THE BERKELEY DIVINITY SCHOOL.

Andover:
WARREN F. DRAPER, PUBLISHER.
MAIN STREET.
1872.

ANDOVER:

PRINTED BY WARREN F. DRAPER.

PRESS, RAND, AVERY, & CO.

CONTENTS.

INTRODUCTION.

Two reasons will account for the appearance of this elementary work. In the first place, ability to read the Hebrew text of the Old Testament is now a requisite for admission to many of our Theological Seminaries; particularly is it required of the candidates for admission to the *Berkeley Divinity School*, for whom this treatise is especially prepared. In many cases — happily becoming less every day, from the increasing interest in Hebrew — the student fruitlessly seeks for some one capable of instructing him in the rudiments of the language, and the task of learning to read the text with the help of a Grammar alone seems a difficult one. And it is indeed difficult, because the Grammars do not treat this matter in sufficient detail, or illustrate it with enough examples. In fact, they do not seem to appreciate the beginner's chief trouble, and so do not provide for it. And yet ten years' experience in teaching this language demonstrates that the fluent reading of the text is one of the greatest difficulties which the learner has to encounter, and which indeed is rarely thoroughly overcome. It is not strange that (1) the unaccustomed forms of the letters; (2) the method of reading from right to left, — backward as it were; (3) the vowels *above, below,* and *in* the line, thus making virtually three lines to be carried in the eye at once ; (4) the vocal and silent sh'vas ; (5) the doubtful vowels, etc.,— in view of all these things, it is not strange that the reading of the text seems to the beginner an arduous task. And yet if it is not perfectly acquired, the student, as he goes on, finds his troubles much increased from his inability to recognize and pronounce at once the printed forms of words.

2. To meet this difficulty is the second reason for the publication of this little book. A thoroughly elementary Grammar, with exercises by way of illustrating each subject presented, was sought for in vain. Most of the Grammars merely give the general principles or abstract rules, with few or no examples to illustrate them. *Kalisch's* Grammar, however (published in England), is constructed on the plan of illustrating the principles with exercises, and so seems to meet the want alluded to better than any other ; but the elementary points are not as fully illustrated in detail as seems desirable. The expense of this Grammar also puts it beyond the reach of most theological students.

The aim of this work is to give the student all that is needful to enable him to read the text of the Old Testament, keeping rigorously to the plan of stating clearly and precisely everything that is *essential* to this purpose. This work is not a *Hebrew Grammar*, but it is a guide and a help to the reading of the text of the Hebrew Bible. One thing is given at a time, with exercises for practice, so that each point may be perfectly comprehended. It is hoped that the book is so constructed as to enable the learner to read the Hebrew text without the services of the living teacher. The author has taken nothing for granted on the part of the student. By a systematic and progressive plan of arrangement, which he *must* follow closely and steadily, he is led on from section to section. *No section must be begun until the preceding one is thoroughly mastered.* Nothing at all is gained by haste or skimming. The exercises under each section are to be written, not merely once or twice, but many times over, until perfect familiarity with the forms and sounds of the characters and signs is acquired.

The exercises should always be read *aloud*, over and over again, until each word can be pronounced at sight, without stammering or hesitation. Fluency of reading will only be the result of constant practice.

In order to write the English words in Hebrew characters the student will be careful to note how each consonant and vowel is represented. The equivalents herein adopted differ somewhat from those which are commonly made use of; e.g. *Tsara* is usually represented by *ē*, which might be pronounced like *e* in *mete*. It is here represented by *ā* as in *fate*, and so is not liable to be pronounced grave, *ä*, or short, *ă*, or like *ee*.

In giving the pronunciation of the *names* of the consonants, of the vowels, and of the other signs affecting the text, phonetic spelling has been adopted, which, though looking awkward to a scholar, will prevent wrong pronunciation on the part of the learner. Wherever *ch* occurs, it is always *hard*, as in *chasm, cholem*. The book is labelled " for beginners," but it is hoped that the advanced scholar will not be able to charge it with inaccuracy or lack of perspicuity.

How far we have succeeded in enabling the student to

read fluently the text of the Hebrew Bible must be ascertained by a *faithful* and *regular* use of the book itself. May it, in its humble way, so have assisted him in laying the foundations of his Hebrew learning, that he may more easily advance in the prosecution of so sacred a study.

MIDDLETOWN, Epiphany, 1872.

GUIDE

READING THE HEBREW TEXT.

§ 1. THE ALPHABET.

HEBREW is written and read from right to
left. The letters, which are twenty-two in
number, are exclusively consonants, though
some of them have also the power of vowels.
These letters, with their respective names and
sounds, are given on page 11.

It will be noticed that two of them, namely,
älĕf and ăyĭn, are represented by no English
equivalent. Ahlĕf is usually likened to the
spiritus lenis (') of the Greeks, or to the *silent*
h in our word *hour*. Hence practically it has
no sound.

The true sound of ăyĭn — which was probably similar to the Arabic *Ain* — is said to be
unpronounceable by our organs of speech. It
is represented in the Septuagint sometimes by
γ, sometimes by the *spiritus asper*, sometimes
by the *spiritus lenis*. Attempts of grammarians

to exhibit its power by, *g, ch, 'h, gn, rg,* etc., merely show the impossibility of adequately representing it.   In the midst of such difficulty and uncertainty of designating its pronunciation, the method of passing it over altogether as having no sound has been adopted, after the example of the German universities, and on the authority of many grammarians.

In the last column of the Table on the opposite page the similar letters are placed side by side, in order that the student, at a glance, may note both their points of resemblance and of difference.

At the bottom of the same column are given the five letters (called *dilatabiles*) which are used in manuscripts and old editions of the Bible in order to avoid the blank space which would otherwise occasionally remain in the line, from the fact that no word is ever allowed to be divided at the end of a line.   Such division is now avoided in modern printing by judicious spacing.

Note 1. — The *names* of the letters are monosyllabic, except those of *ahlef, geemel, dahleth, zayin, lahmeth, sahmek,' ayin,* and *tsahthay.*

Note 2. — The learner can acquire familiarity with the forms and sounds of these letters only by writing them down, and uttering the sound of each as often as he writes it.   This practice *must be persisted in* until each consonant can be recognized with facility, and pronounced readily and without the slightest hesitation.

Finals	Form	Sound	Name	Equivalent in this book	Similarity of Shape
	א	Scarcely audible breathing.	Ah'-lĕf	א	כ ב
	בּ	b	} Bayth	b	
	כ	v (bh)		v	ג נ
	ג or ג	g always hard, as in go	Gee'-mĕl	g	
	דּ	d	} Dah'-lĕth	d	ך ר ד
	ד	th as in those		th	
	ה	h as in he	Hay	h	ה ה ת
	ו	v	Vahv	v	ין ו י
	ז	z	Ză'-yĭn	z	
	ח	ch as in German, nach	Chayth	ch	ם מ ט
	ט	t	Tayth	t	
	י	y	Yōthe	y	ם ס
ך	כ or כ	k	Kăf	k	
	ל	l	Lah'-mĕth	l	ע צ ע
ם	מ	m	Maim	m	ש ש
ן	נ	n	Noon	n	
	ס	s as in so	Sah'-mĕk	s	
	ע	No sound	Ă'-yĭn	y	Dilated.
	פּ	p	} Pay	p	
ף	פ	f (ph)		f	ן ן ן
ץ	צ	ts as in nets	Tsah'-thay	ts	
	ק	k	Kōfe	k	ך ך ך
	ר	r	Raysh	r	
	שׁ	sh	Sheen	sh	ם ן ך
	שׂ	s like ס	Seen	s	
	תּ	t	} Tahv	t	ך
	ת	th as in thin		th	

Rem. 1. These characters are *Chaldee*, not Hebrew. The proper Hebrew letters are found only on monuments and coins.

Rem. 2. In writing these characters, observe that the horizontal strokes are heavy, while the perpendicular ones are light.

Rem. 3. The *letters* and their *sounds* are first to be thoroughly learnt, and afterwards their *names* should be acquired.

2. It will be noted that each of the letters *k, s, t, th,* and *v* have *two* equivalents in Hebrew. The learner will therefore carefully note that when the following Hebrew letters are intended to be expressed, the English equivalents in the Exercises are printed in *italics*.

ק, *k*;   ס, *s*;   ט, *t*;   ד, *th*;   ב, *v*.

3. As certain of the letters closely resemble each other, the beginner must take care not to confound ב with כ; ג with נ; ד with ר; ד with ך; ה with ח; ח with ת; ה with ת; ו with ר; ו with י; ו with ז; ז with נ; ו with ן; ט with מ; ם with ס; ע with צ; ע with ץ; שׁ with שׂ.

What is the difference in form between Dahleth and final Kaf? between Zayin and final Noon? Hay and Chayth? Vahv and final Noon? Chayth and Tahv? Bayth and Kaf? Hay and Tahv? Geemel and Noon? Samek and final Maim? Dahleth and Raysh? Ayin and final Tsah*th*ay? Vahv and Yo*th*e? Vahv and Raysh? Ayin and Tsa*th*ay? Sheen and Seen?

Rem. The dot over שׁ and שׂ is called the *Diacritical Point.*

4. When Kaf, Maim, Noon, Pay, or Tsah*th*ay

occur at the *end of words*, they are written as in the column headed " Final."

5. In Hebrew the letters and words follow each other *from right to left*. Thus our word MOUTH, written Hebrew-wise, would be HTUOM.

NOTE.— TH must be represented by ד or ת, not by טה; SH by ש, never by סה; TS by צ, never by טס.

EXERCISE I.

Write in Hebrew characters the following consonants:

[When either M, N, K, F, or TS occurs at the end of words in this and other Exercises, take care to give it its "final" form.]

B, r, sh, th, l, h, y, m, ts, *v*, ch, p, n, r, f, *th*, *t*, k, sh, z, g, ts, v, k, *s*, d, r, *k*, ts final, k, m, s, th, ch, *th*, r, b, h, n, *v*, l, y, *t*, sh, g, t, k, d, s, n final, z, m, p, ts, y, b, th, m final, *k*, *s*, g, r, f final, d, th, *t*, l, k final, y, z, v, b, s, t, g, h, k, f, p, *th*, *k*, *v*, n, r, b, ts, th, ch, h, g, *t*, z, d, s, l, n, f, *th*, m, s, k, ch, *v*, *k*, ptr, yms, yhn, mth, mrk, lk, hbrvs, thslns, lyh, *t*rm, *th*sn, m*s*s, dkf, tschy, shpl, prf, rts*v*, shrg, chshl, hshm, hlk, btsm, yhvh, mshp*t*, ts*thk*h, gzl, gthl, my*th*, ythvm, kmn, kmv, lmnk, *k*lm, *k*rv, sprts, bchn, rchf, shlf, brk, srh, vrhm, vksh*v*, ytschk, ysrl, dn, krch, shmn, yh*th*, rchl, sh*v*l, l*t*n, blhn, b*t*n, srg, y*k*shn, *k*tn, mzmr, mktl, sn.

NOTE. — This Exercise should be written many times, until perfect familiarity with the forms and sounds is acquired.

EXERCISE II.

Write the English equivalents for the consonants in Genesis i., see p. 45, passing over א
and ע when they occur, as having no sound.
Practice both writing and pronouncing the
consonants in this chapter until any and every
letter can be pronounced at sight.

NOTE. — The learner ought not to go on to the following exercises until he is as thoroughly familiar with the forms and sounds
of the letters of the Hebrew alphabet as he is with his own A B C.

§ 2. THE VOWELS.

I. THE LONG VOWELS.

1. For convenience and simplicity we may
divide the vowels into two classes, viz. five long
and five short.   The long vowels are:

		Sounded as	Represented by
Käh'-mĕts	ָ,	ä in father,	ä
Tsāy'-rāy	ֵ or יֵ,	ā in fate,	ā
Chee'-rĕk	יִ,	ee in feet,	ee
Chō'-lĕm	וֹ or ֹ,	ō in over,	ō
Shoo'-rĕk	וּ,	oo in fool,	oo

NOTE. — The horizontal line represents the consonant to which
the vowel belongs; ┬ means, therefore, that the vowel ˎ stands
beneath the consonant; ┴ that the vowel stands over the consonant.
Ch should be pronounced hard, as in chasm.

2. The vowels are mostly pronounced after
the consonant under which they stand, e.g.
בָּ = bä ; בֵּי = bā ; מָ = mā ; כִּי = kee.

When *cholem* (*defectively* written ֹ) *follows* a consonant it is placed *over* it, e.g. בֹ = bō; פֹ = pō; דֹר = dōr.

Cholem (*fully* written וֹ) and Shoorek וּ, stand *in the line* with the other consonants, e.g. קוֹם = kōm; קוּם = koom.

EXERCISE III.

Pronounce, and write in English letters the following Hebrew syllables.

[As älef and ăyin have no sound, they may, for the sake of convenience, be represented by a dash (thus אָם may be written –ām; מָצָא = mätsä–; עָשׂוּ = –äsoo; מֵעַל = mā–äl, etc.), or they may be left unexpressed.]

בָּ ,בֹ ,הָ ,הִי ,הוֹ ,גֵּי ,גּוֹ ,בֵּ ,זוּ ,זִי ,פוֹ ,פִי ,לָ,

לוֹ ,בִּי ,רָ ,סֵי ,מִי ,מָ ,מוֹ ,נוּ ,שֶׁ ,שָׁ ,כ ,רִי ,ר ,תִּי,

טֵי ,עָ ,צוּ ,קוֹ ,מֵי ,אַ ,אָ ,לוֹ ,רָ ,יוֹ ,הוּ ,חֵי ,חָ ,פֵי,

דִי ,לֵ ,כֵּי ,שָׂ ,סוּ ,נִי ,נָ ,נוּ ,שִׁי ,דָ ,דֵי ,עוֹ ,כּוֹ ,כָּ,

לֵי ,סִי ,אוֹ ,רוּ ,קָ ,עִי ,כּוּ ,נִי ,בֵי ,טָ ,טוּ ,מ ,חִי ,זָ,

צֵי ,יוּ ,יֵי ,הוּ ,סִי ,רֵ ,שׁוֹ ,דָ ,תֵ ,פִי ,מוּ ,לִי ,חוֹ ,וִי,

ווֹ ,גִּי ,עָ ,עוֹ ,רָ ,יֹ ,קִי ,בָ ,הוּ ,לוֹ ,טֵ ,רוּ ,כָּ ,כ ,כוּ,

קָ ,פִי ,גֵּי ,נוּ ,מֵ ,רָ ,לִי ,לוֹ ,שֶׁ ,בּוּ ,חָ ,כִּי ,ה ,לוֹ,

בִּי ,עוֹ ,רָ ,הִי ,וִי ,הֵי ,חוֹ ,יִי ,יֵי ,זֹ ,אָ ,אִי ,כֵּי ,ה,

תֵ ,טוּ ,מוֹ ,רִי ,סוּ ,יוֹ ,יוּ ,אֹ ,חִי ,מוּ ,פָ ,תוֹ ,קִי ,ס,

שִׂי ,נָ ,עִי ,רוּ ,תֵ ,כּוֹ ,לָ ,ל ,צִי ,רִי ,נוּ ,גּוּ.

EXERCISE IV.

Pronounce and write in English letters the
following Hebrew words.

דָג , קָם , קוּם ,גַּב , דֹב , מוּם , גּוּר , שָׁם , מֵת , כֹּל ,

לָן , אֶת , אִישׁ , הוֹד , יָם , יוֹד , כּוּר , נֹב , סוּס , גִּיל , תֹּךְ ,

שֵׁם , קוּב , טוֹב , דָּם , בּוּשׁ , לָז , יִיף , אִי , הֵם , תּוּץ , גֵּז ,

הוּר , שֵׁן , קוּן , טָשׁ , דִּין , בֶּן , גָּד , בֵּית , לוּב , יוֹר , יֵט ,

כּוּס , אַל , אוּן , חֵת , רָם , עִיר , עָב , דֹב , זוּל , הוֹד ,

מִין , גּוֹב , מוּשׁ , יָשׁ , כָּה , חוֹב , דִּין , דָּל , גִּיר , אָב , טָל ,

צֹר , צֵן , קוֹץ , עוֹז , תֹּף , דָל , הוּץ , הוִי , חָי , אוֹב ,

כִּים , גִּישׁ , חוֹר , נָא , נוֹב , כִּיס , כִּית , אוֹת , רִיב , פּוּט ,

טִים , שׁוֹם , פֵּז , טוֹב , זָג , סֹךְ , בָּז , בֵּל , שֵׁיךְ , שִׂיד ,

אֵל , כִּיס , לֹג , לֹד , נֵיר , סִיג , סִיס , הוֹר , אוֹר , רִיב ,

עֹט , הֹם , חֵיק , נוֹב , זִיד , גֵּר , דּוּץ , צִיל , עָב , מִיץ ,

קוֹץ , גֹג , מוּת , זִיף , דּוּג , כּוּר , מֹף , דַּךְ , קָץ , קִים , הוּל ,

לוּט , נֹף , טוּל , רִיק , פּוּג , יוֹב , שָׁד , חֵץ , רִיק , הוּם ,

נִיר , לָז , סֹף , סוּף , בָּז , בָּן , שָׂר , תִּין , הָם , נוּם.

EXERCISE V.

Pronounce the following Hebrew words.

שָׁתוּל , מָצוֹר , עָמֵל , הָמָן , בָּלָק , פָּנִים , שָׁרֹק ,

תּוֹמִים , רוֹצֵץ , עֹבֵד , מֵשָׁא , מֵעִים , יָכֹל , נוֹלָד , יוֹרָם ,

, דֹּנֶג, דָּוִיד, גִּיחוֹן, גֵּשָׁן, גָּצֶק, בָּצֶק, עֵיטָם, אָפִיל, אֹפִיל, אָפִיר, יָרֵא

, הֶסֶב, הוּסָב, סָדִין, סִיחוֹן, סִינָן, עוֹרֵב, עֵילָם, חֵזוּ

, מָשׁוֹשׁ, מֵיתִים, הַלּוֹן, חוּפָם, הֵבִין, יָבִין, בָּחִיר

, אָשׁוּר, אָנֹכִי, אֵילוֹן, אָים, אִילָן, הֵאִיר, כּוּמָז, נָכוֹן

, כּוּשִׁי, כּוּשָׂרָה, מוֹעָד, מֹפֶת, הֵמִיק, יָנִין, נֹצָה, וָוֵי

, יָמִים, פֹּחֵן, נָדִיב, גּוֹזָן, בֵּנִי, מָזָר, טָנַף, דָּיֵק, בֶּרֶד

, בִּיתָן, לָשׁוֹן, יוֹנֵק, שֶׁגָל, מָחוּז, טָמוּן, שָׂעִיר, קָטָן

, דִּיבוֹן, בָּצֶק, לָהֶם, יָכֹן, יוֹקִים, יָיבָשׁ, קְטָל, לַעַג

, יוֹרִים, יָדוֹן, יֵיטִיב, הָלָב, יוֹשָׁב, מוּשִׁי, עָשָׁן, אָמֹץ

, הָכָל, הֵילָל, תָּמָר, צָנֵם, תּוֹעֵבָה, שָׂעִיר, קָטָן, דָּנִים.

NOTE. — The learner will practice upon each of these Exercises until each word can be pronounced at sight.

EXERCISE VI.

Write in Hebrew characters the following syllables and words, taking care to write from right to left.

Bä, dä, *vee*, sō, lā, mee, noo, gā, shoo, *kä*, bee, chō, hoo, *th*ā, lō, see, nō, pä, *t*ō, yee, zoo, mä, tsä, yā, hō, fä, vä, chee, tā, lee, koo, rō, *t*ä, gō, yū, shā, dee, hä, yō, nā, moo, lä, yoo, kee, tsō, fee, zä, vee, loo, *k*ō, *s*ā, nō, roo, kō, shä, chä, tee, *t*ä, shō, bän, bōn, loon, däg, kōl, dän, bāth, väv, tseets, shoom, geesh, yāz, cheel, mān, keer, gōl, chäth, tsoor, zäk, yäm, mōts, meets, *t*āth, yō*th*,

där, nāts, loog, pool, bäl, bōs, seen, *k*āts, lool,
däth, chāk, hōn, rā*k*, reev, pōth, book, läz,
cheesh, bōr, *t*oo*v*, cho*k*, lā*v*, där, moo*t*, seer,
sōk, tāl, yäth, *k*äm, moosh, ‫ע‬ool, ‫ע‬ōf, ‫ע‬äz, ‫א‬āv,
‫א‬ōn, ‫א‬oo*th*, mām, noon, ‫א‬äch, ‫א‬ām, rāsh, ‫ע‬ō*th*,
sheen, ‫ע‬är, ‫ע‬oor, tär, dō*v*, hān, pook, gän, been,
shoo*v*, booz, *t*ool, päts, neef, yōm.

Write in Hebrew characters the following
words.

Kāthoo*v*, täshā*v*, bänoo, yächāl, täree*th*,
täfook, näkoom, härāts, yāshā*v*, shäleem,
bōhoo, *k*ä*t*ōl, chā*th*äsh, māleets, neesän, tōhoo,
bārāk, shälōm, yālāk, *k*ōlōth, yä*k*oom, *k*ōmäh,
reeshōn, rā*k*eem, büsär, yōthār, hā*t*ee*v*, hōlee*th*,
yämeem, yōnā*k*, yä*k*är, käleel, nä*v*āl, nōsū*s*,
hāneef, zūthän, zäkoor, sheerünoo, tä*k*eemoo,
mārächo*k*, hōlee*th*ō, rä*th*äfoo, yōnä*k*eem, oovä-
nōth, yä*k*eemoo, tōfäfōth, yōzä*v*ä*th*, kōkä*v*eem,
härüree, yōyüree*v*, yōchänän, bämōthä, süree-
geem, sookäthee, sheeräthānoo, tōshee*v*änee.

3. When ‫א‬ is unprovided with a vowel sign,
and follows *any* long vowel, it merely serves to
prolong the sound of such vowel: e.g. ‫בָּרָא‬ =
bärä ; ‫תֵּצֵא‬ = tātsā ; ‫בּוֹא‬ = bō ; ‫קָרִיא‬ = *k*äree ;
‫נָשׂוּא‬ = näsoo.

ה may serve the same purpose, when it
stands at the *end of a word*, after ָ , ֶ , ֵ
[or ֹ § 2. II.], e.g. גָּלָה = gälä, גָּלֶה = gälā, גָּלֹה ·
= gälō.

We have already seen that י, having no
vowel of its own, after ֵ or ִ simply serves to
make the prolonged sound of the vowel Tsārā
or Cheerĕk; and that ו, with no vowel under
it, or immediately preceding it, loses its con-
sonantal power entirely, and becomes a mere
holder of the vowel ֹ. These letters therefore
quiesce or rest in the following vowels:

א in *any* vowel;

ה in ָ , ֶ , ֵ , ֹ ;

ו in וֹ or וּ ;

י in יִ or יֵ (or יֶ § 2. II. Obs. 3).

4. But when either of these letters is provided with a vowel sign, it must be regarded
as a *consonant;* e.g. in אָשׁוּב, א, as it has a
vowel under it, must be a consonant; so in הֵן,
ה must be a consonant; so in צַיִד, יֶלֶד, וַזָּר,
the Vav and Yo*the* are consonants. (cf. § 9, 1.)

EXERCISE VIII.

Pronounce the following words; and in each
case state whether the א, ה, ו, or י is quiescent
or not.

בְּאֵר , בָּא , בּוֹא , לֹא , נֵצֵא , מָה , נָא , פֶּה , הוּא , הִיא

רֹאשׁ , לִי , הֵטִיב , שׁוֹבוּ , נָצָא , קָשָׁה , רֹאשׁ , לֵאמֹר ,

פּוּעָה , טָאטָא , קָאם , צֵאת , יֵתֵא , בְּדָאם , יָרֵא , יֹאכַל ,

פֵּארֹת , נָאוָה , רֹאשׁוֹן , דָּאג , רָאבמוֹת , רֹאשׁ , יָנֵאץ , זֹאת ,

פֹּראת , פָּארֶן , פֹּא , פֵּאה , לֵכָה , מָבוֹא , אָבִיא , טָמֵאת ,

צֵאה , כְּלַאתֵי , חֹטֵא , מוֹצִיא , תְּבֹאת , קֹרֵא , נָאה , גֵוָה ,

הָיָה , רָוֶה , אָתָא , וָאִיץ , נָיוֹת , יָנֵי , יוֹנֵק , דָּיֵק , הָנָה ,

תָּאִים , שָׁאֹג , קָרָאת , יֹאבֵד , הָכִיל , קָרָה , יֵהוּא , סוֹא ,

נָשִׂיא , נֹאד , הָגָה לָאט , יוֹדָא , לָבִיא , מוֹאָב , סָלוּא ,

נָבִיא , יוֹיָרִיב , לֵוִיָּא ·

5. (*a*) When Cholem (without וֹ) follows שׂ, or precedes שׁ, it *coincides with the diacritical point* of these letters, the single dot serving both as the vowel ō, and as determining the sound of שׁ, so that בֹּשׁ = bōsh, for בֹּשׁ; שֹׂם = sōm, for שֹׂם.

(*b*) If Cholem (defectively written) follows שׁ, or precedes שׂ, it is written over *the opposite arm*; so that שֹׁד = shōth ; עֹשָׂה = ᵓōsā.

EXERCISE IX.

Write in Hebrew characters the following words (ō in every instance to be written *defectively*, i.e. with the simple ִ).

Chōsān, chōshān, yōshāv, shōlām, chäsōf,

täfōs, shōfā*t*, sōrōk, mōshāk, shōrōs, shōrāts,
shälōsh, shōkā*v*, *k*ōsh*t*, nōsāא, nōshāא, shōץāl,
ץōsäh, ץōshār, tōshee*v*, sōkār, yäshōm, shōmām,
sōnāא, näshōs, shōץär, sōrāf, yäshō*k*, shōkān,
nōshā*k*, gōshee, sōrā*k*, mōshāväh, kōshāl, sōkāk,
yōshānā, pärōsh, shō*v*ee, meeshōr, shōkākäh,
dōshāsh, täshō*v*näh, bōshäshoo, yä*k*ōshtee.

EXERCISE X.

Pronounce and write in English characters
the following words.

NOTE. — When not preceded by a vowel שׂ = ōsh; שׁ = ōs.
When שׁ has no vowel *under* it שׂ = sō; שׁ = shō, except at the *end
of words*, when it is ōs.

טֹם , וָשֹׁד, יִבְשׁוּ , סֹן , יָקֹשׁ , שֹׁךְ , אֹשֶׁר , שׂוֹרֵק, סֹכֶן

רָמֹשׁ , עָשׂר , טֹנָא , טֹךְ , יָשֹׁחוּ , מָקֹשׁ , מֹשֵׁל , שֹׁפֶר , בֹּשׁ ,

אָשֹׁת , פֶּרֹשׁ , טֹרֹשׁ , טֹרֹשׁ , חָרֹשׁ , יָשֹׁד , כָּשֹׁשׁ , פָּתֹל ,

יְתִיב , יָבֹשׁ , שֹׁכָה , שֹׁרֹדוּ , אֹשֶׁב , בֹּסֹס , הָשֹׁךְ , חָסֹךְ ,

גֹּשׁוּ , יָשֹׁךְ , שֹׁרֵר , שֹׁתָה , יָשֹׁר , שֹׁרֵר , שָׁשֹׁן , עֲשֹׁנִי ,

שָׁלֹשׁ , טֹטֶר , עָשֹׁךְ , בֹּשֹׁשׁ , חֹשֶׁךְ , טֹאָס ,

חֹשֶׁךְ , יָשֹׁק , נֶשֹׁק , יָדֹשׁ , חָשֹׁף , יָשֹׁב , טֹטֶט , שֹׁרֹשׁ ,

בֹּשֹׁל , קֹשֶׁשׁ , שֹׁנוֹת , עֹשָׂה , נָשָׂא , נָשֹׂא , יָשֹׁכוּ , שֹׁדֵד ,

עֹשׂוּ , נֹטֶב , עָשֹׁק , הֹשֵׁב , יָשֹׁלוּ .

NOTE. — The student should not go on to the following Exercises
until he has perfectly mastered the principles already presented.
Thoroughness cannot be too often or too strongly insisted upon.

II. The short vowels are:

		Sounded as	Represented by
Păt'-tăch	ָ֯	ă in dăsh,	ă
Sĕg'-ōl	ֱ	ĕ in mĕt,	ĕ
Chee'-rĕk	ִ	ĭ in pĭn,	ĭ
Kä'-mĕts Chä-toof	ָ	ŏ in hŏt,	ŏ
Kĭb'-boots	ֻ	ŭ in fŭll,	ŭ

Rem. 1. Cheerek, ִ, and Kibboots, ֻ, in *open* (§ 4. 2) or in *accented* syllables are, however, *long*.

Rem. 2. Kamets (broad ä) and Kamets Chatoof (short ŏ) have the same form; the rule for distinguishing the one from the other will be given further on (§ 8).

Rem. 3. Segol sometimes quiesces in י, and hence assumes the form ֶי.

Rem. 4. Pattach and Segol at the *end of words* quiesce with ה; e.g. מָה = mă; שֶׁה = sĕ.

EXERCISE XI.

Pronounce and write in English characters the following syllables.

Note. — In this Exercise ָ is short ŏ.

הַת , הֹן , גַד , הֶל , גַל , אַב , הַל , זֶה , גֶשׁ , לַן , פֶּן , רַב ,

בַּז , יַם , עַם , פֶּה , אֶל , הַד , אַף , אַך , בֶּן , עַל , אִם , סַל ,

בֶּן , טַל , הֶק , חַג , קֶם , זֶה , הֶם , קַר , הַר , יַק , לַשׁ , גֻּל ,

גַּל ; קֶט , טַל , נַם , קָשׁ , קַר , לַף , אֶם , עַב , חַס , כַּת ,

נַג , לֶן , הַנ , וַף , נַט , הֶק , נַט , בֶּן , כֶּם , אֶת , יַל , תַּק , הַב ,

הַל , מָשׁ , בַּן , קָן , מִן , יַת , מֶל , נַח , רֶץ , צַד , שָׁם ,

אַב , חַץ , צַד , תֶּם , כַּל , זַף , קַב , בֶּץ , רֶן , הַב , גַּב , מַם ,

,מֵד ,כָּל ,שֶׁב ,זַד ,מֵר ,קֶם ,שָׁט ,לֶף ,סַק ,הֵם ,קַח

,שָׁק ,טֶב ,תֵּס ,יֵק ,קַל ,שֶׁר ,טַן ,אֶק ,תֵּל ,יַף ,יֵת

,קֵר ,יַד ,דֵּן ,בַּר ,מֵל ,חָד ,מַת ,מֵה ,נֵס ,בְּג ,לַל ,אַן

,סָב ,אֹה ,נַף ,רַק ,מֵל ,צֵם ,לֵךְ ,קָט ,תֵּר ,שָׁב ,בַּר

,הֵם ,מֵךְ ,אַג ,לֵב ,תֵּם ,מַל ,נֵר ,פֵּךְ ,רֵק ,הֵז ,טַן

,נֵם ,בֵּל ,דַּד ,בֵּךְ ,אַט ,פֵּט ,שֵׁב ,סָל ,הַן ,זַל ,טֵץ ,תֵּה

,יָה ,רֵב ,עַד ,רָק ,טֵן ,כֵּב.

EXERCISE XII.

Pronounce and write in English characters the following words.

NOTE.—In this Exercise the student will pay no attention to this mark, $_\tau$; but write and pronounce the word as if it were absent altogether; e.g. מַלְכָּה = mălkäh. $_\tau$ herein is not short ŏ.

אָבָר ,בֶּטַח ,עֹשֶׁר ,יָרֵב ,קֶרַח ,נֹעַם ,אָרֶץ ,בֶּלַע

,עָשֶׁךְ ,אֶסְכֹּל ,מִגְרָשׁ ,יֶטַע ,בַּעַם ,נָאַם ,קָצוּ ,מִשְׁעָב

,יִקְטֹל ,יִרְאַת ,אֶסֶת ,שֹׂסֶה ,כֹּבֶד ,הִגְלִי ,חֶסְפַס ,יַנְהֵנִי

,עֵזֶר ,עִבְרִית ,טֹרֶט ,שִׂמְךָ ,חַדִים ,יֶחְסַר ,הֹמֶץ ,חֶזְקָה

,זֵכֶר ,תָּוֶךְ ,טֹאַת ,גִּלְגַּל ,חַרְצַר ,אֲמָלָל ,גַּרְזֶן ,עַפְעַה

,יִשְׁבִּי ,יֵשֶׁב ,יָשַׁב ,יִרְאֶה ,יָקֶם ,הוֹצַח ,יַחְדֹּו ,יוֹנֶקֶת

,טַלְטֵל ,כַּרְמֶל ,כַּרְכֹּב ,בַּסְלָחִים ,כֶּסֶל ,כָּלְמַד ,הַכְלִילֹו

,בַּלְפֵל ,נִבְזָה ,יֵשֶׁר ,פַּרְעֹשׁ ,גֶּפֶן ,פִּתְהָה ,יִפְטֹט

,פַּרְשֶׁגֶן ,יִפְרֹט ,פַּרְבַּר ,עֲרָוַת ,מֶכְשָׁל ,אֶסְלַח ,יִתְמַרְמַר

קִלְקֵל, מְשֻׁלֶכֶת, הֻשְׁלַךְ, מֻפְקָד, לִשְׁכָּה, מַרְאַת, מַרְאֶה,

סִפְתֵיהֶם, דִּמְכֶם, קַרְדֹּם, רֲחַק, אַרְמוֹן, מִגְרָשׁ, בֹּקֶר,

יֶדְכֶם, טֶבַח, נִשְׁבֶּרֶת, יָפֶה, סִלְסֵל, פֻּרְפֵּר, גֶּשֶׁשׁ,

עִבְרִים, אָנַן, קִלְקֵל, לַהַט, הַסְפֵּן, תִּתְעַרְעַר, כַּרְסֵם,

עֶבְרִים, תִּשְׁעַת, עֶדְיוֹ, מֻפְקָד, מְשֻׁלֶכֶת, גִּלְנַּל, יוֹנֶיהָ,

מֶקְרַח, אוֹנֶיךָ, גֵּרֵשׁ, הֻשְׁלַךְ, בְּרֻפֹּתֶיהָ, הַסְנֶה, מֶכְשַׁל,

בֵּלֶיךָ, סִפְרוּ, עָלֶיהָ, הַרְחַק, קֵמְעוּ, צִמְתֻּנִי, יִשְׁתֶּה,

מִמְשַׁלְתּוֹ, הִשְׁאַלְתִּיהוּ, הִתְטוֹטַטְנָה.

EXERCISE XIII.

Write · in Hebrew characters the following syllables and words.

Dăg, mĭn, găth, pĕn, kăf, păch, dăm, chŏk, shăth, kŏl, găn, yă*th*, zĭv, bĭn, kĕn bŭn, dĕl, zŭm, dĭv, dŭn, hĭm, hŭl, săl, dăth, hăr, gĕl, yĭz, yĭsh, păth, yĕsh, nĭr, אĕl, אăk, אĭm, אĭsh, עĭm, עăm, עŭn, עĭl, עŭv, tsĭn, răts, shĕv, gĕsh, rĭv, nĕ-fĕsh, mĕ-lĕk, gă*th*ăl, *k*ătăl, *k*ō*th*ĕsh, lăhĕm, băkĕm, rĕ-gĕl, mōrăg, chălĕ*k*, dĕ-rĕk, tăfĕn, tsĭmdā, kŏvnō, shooshăn, shăkăv, shōmrăh, tĭ*k*tōl, tămăk, tŏ*k*tăl, kĕ-lĕv, dălyoo, bŏtsrăh, hŭshkăv, mŭ*k*răch, tăchmō*th*, mĭk-nĕh, yĭglĕh, yăyĭn, părăsh, mōshĕh, yăvăn, mĕ-lăch, lĕ-chĕm, nătsăl, chōshĕk, mŭkdăsh, sĭfrā, mălkee, yĭn-tăn, gŭ*th*lō, chĕvrōn, rĭshpā, nĭstär, năfshee, bĭrkăth, chŭfshee, bătĕn, kĭlyōth, yĭrbĕh, bĭl-

văv, tăchtĕkä, אֵלׄקׄōshee, măzlāg, mĭshmĕrĕth, mĭshpăchtō, hōrăᵗʰtĕm, shĭmshōn, yĭschăₜ, shĭk-mee, hŏnchăl, kŭrbăl, hăftsăr, chŏfzee, pŏlpăl, bĭltee, אֵthkĕm, אōsĭfkä, shŏvrānee, sĭksăktä, hŏthdăshnäh, tĭmshōlnäh, hĭthrăchătstee, tĭth-chălchăl, tĭthmōgăgnäh.

§ 3.   THE SH'VA.

1. Every consonant which — standing at the *beginning* or in the *middle* of a word — has no vowel, and is not a quiescent letter (§ 2, 3), is provided with a sign to indicate the *absence* of a vowel.

2. A consonant at the *end* of a word does not take this sign, unless it be preceded by another vowelless letter.

Exc. Final Kaph (ך), however, when it has no vowel, always takes the sign.

3. This sign has the form of our colon, ⃜, and is placed under a letter, thus בְּ. and is called *simple Sh'va.*

4. Simple Sh'va may be either *vocal* or *silent.*

(*a*) It is always *vocal* under the *first* letter of a *word*; e.g. תְּמוֹל = t'mōl.

(*b*) It is always *silent* under the *last* letter of a *word*; e.g. אָתְ = אăt.

(*c*) *Both sh'vas* under the *two final* letters of a word are *silent*; e.g. קָטַלְתְּ = *k*ătălt.

4

(*d*) In the *middle* of a word it is sometimes vocal, sometimes silent.

(1.) If preceded by an unaccented *short* vowel it is *silent*.

(2.) It is, however, *vocal* if preceded by

(*a*) an unaccented *long* vowel;

(*b*) another sh'va;

(*c*) Dägesh Forte (§ 5, 2, 3);

(*d*) Metheg (§ 7, 3);

(*e*) *Väv conversive, וַ;

(*f*) the *Article, הַ; or,

(*g*) if it stands between two similar letters,

NOTE. —* These occur only at the *beginning of words*; e.g. וַיְהִי is to be read vă-y'-hee, not văy-hee; הַיְסוֹר = hă-y'-*soth*, not hăy-*soth*.

(*e*) If two Sh'vas occur in the *middle* of a word, the first is silent, the second is sounded.

5. The *sound* of vocal Sh'va is that of the very short ĕ in *mystery*, or in *catechism*. Fix the lips to pronounce a consonant, e.g. b, p, or t, open the mouth, gently exhale the breath, and the sound of Sh'va is produced. It is, in fact, just enough of a sound to get a letter out of the mouth. *Plane*, in Hebrew, would be written פְּלֶן; *kree* = קְרִי; *bloom* = בְּלוּם.

REM. 1. *Vocal* Sh'va in the exercises is represented thus ('); e.g. בְּךָ = B'kä. *Silent* Sh'va (the mere syllable divider) is *not* designated in the exercises; e.g. yĭmlŏk must be written יִמְלֹךְ. נִכְתַּב would be expressed by nĭktăv.

Rem. 2. It may simplify the matter of determining vocal from silent Sh'va in the *middle* of a word, to remember that *after an un-accented short vowel, or an accented long one,* Sh'va is generally *silent ;* in other cases it is almost always *vocal.*

Rem. 3. An aspirate (§ 5, 1) without Dagesh Lene (§ 5, 1) shows that the preceding Sh'va is *vocal.*

6. The *compound* Sh'vas (which are chiefly used with the guttural letters, viz. עהחא) are :

Chä'-tĕf Păttăch, ⟋, very short ă, as in *Germany.*

Chä'-tĕf Sĕg'-ōl, ⟋, very short ĕ, as in *imbecile.*

Chä'-tĕf Kä'-mĕts, ⟋, very short ŏ, as in *ivory.*

These compound Sh'vas are *always vocal*; and will be represented in the exercises by a small *a, e,* or *o* written above the line ; e.g., חֲלִיפָה = ch^aleefäh ; בְּחֻרִי = bŏch^oree ; יֶחֱזַק = yĕch^ezăk.

EXERCISE XIV.

Write in Hebrew characters the following words, taking care to put in the *silent* as well as the vocal Sh'vas.

B'nā, b'yă *th*, l'yōm, l'meenō, l'kä, k'shōr, m'leets, s'kăn, l'*v*oosh, d'*v*ăr, l'chee, y'fōth, z'măn, v'lō, g'*th*ōl, v'găm, א^emōr, lŏch^olee, s'nĕh, *y*^a*th*ĕn, tĕא^e-läf, h^eyäh, א^emăts, mī*th*yän, yĭtschä*k*, shōr'reem, hăl'loo, lōm'*th*eem, bĭrchäthee, dälthä, zĭlpäh, bĭlhäh, hĭmleek, shŭlchăn, hăy'אōr, lä*y*^amō*th*, ch^alōm, shälächtee, *k*ä*t*ălt, närd, yĭsräאāl, nĭm-r'tsoo, y'hōväh, shŏmräh, א^achōz, א^enō*k*, n'tsōr, bärăkt, yärd, ră*v*t, hĭn'noo, văy'*v*ärĕk, bĭltee, nāl'käh, yāl'kee, t'sōv'vee, ᵊᵃmōräh, vǎy'thäv, k'thǎvteev, yāvk, mĕrchäk, mōlkee, mŭktär, sĭksäkt, yǎft, hᵃlĭthrōsh, אᵉthōm, chᵃnōk, chᵒthäsheem, rōm'moo, m'shōℓteem, shōtᵃtoo, sǎrtĕm, yĭr'אoo, yĭkr'voo, tǎshk, v'hĭthkälkält v'hĭshtǎchᵃveethä.

EXERCISE XV.

Pronounce the following words; also state which of the Sh'vas occurring in each word are *vocal*, and which *silent;* and for what reasons.

בְּעַד ,גּוּעַ ,דְּבַשׁ ,קַמְתָּ ,יֶהְבְּ ,בָּךְ ,אֵת ,תּוֹךְ ,נוֹשְׁבוּ,

נָגְשׁוּ ,גְּאָלוּ ,סָגַרְתְּ ,מַמְטִיר ,קְטַלַתְכֶם ,נִסְגְּרָה ,וּלְמִקְוֵה,

וַיְצַו ,בְּנֶגְדּוּ ,יַדְרְכוּ ,יַד ,יִפְתַּח ,קְרִי ,יְפַצְפְּצֵנִי ,שָׁרְרֵךְ,

חָדַר ,יְפַרְפְּרֵנִי ,יֵטְטְ ,קֹלֵךְ ,הוֹצֵאת ,הַיְאֹר ,הֲמִיתֶךָ,

הַמְלַךְ ,הִתְמַהְמָהֵנוּ ,יָפִי ,מִזְעָזֶיךָ ,הֲמָרִים ,בְּאֶשְׂרִים,

אֲרָחוֹת ,תְּבָרְכוּ ,אֶחֱזוּ ,קְטָלָה ,דִּבְרֵי ,יָרֵא ,וְאֶרְאֶה,

וּרְהָבָה ,קְשֹׁט ,כּוֹהֲבִים ,מַמְלֶכֶת ,יַלְדֵי ,יֵשְׁתְּ ,נַחַתְּ,

צָעֱקִי ,אֱמֹד ,וְאִם ,וַאֲנִי ,לְבַבְךְ ,פָּקַח ,קְטָלָה,

לֵילָה ,מַרְאָשֹׁת ,תְּהוֹם ,לְבִיָּה ,קְנֵז ,עֲרָב ,בָּאֲנִי,

אֲנַחְנוּ ,יְשֵׁנוּ ,סִבְכֵי ,יַקְטִיל ,מִרְדָּף ,מְהָיוֹת ,תַּדְשֵׁא,

שׁוֹנַאֲךָ ,יְהְיֶה ,שְׁנֵי ,וַיְשָׁרֶת ,לְכִי ,אֶהְיֶה ,אֱלֹהִים,

אַחֲרֵי ,יְהִי ,הַמְשֹׁל ,וַיְמַהֵר ,לַעֲשֹׁת ,תַּשְׂכִּיל ,הַמְמַלְאִים,

אֲשֶׁר ,יְהֹוָה ,אֲדָמָה ,הִתְבָּרַכְתָּ ,בְּנִי ,עֲנִי ,הַצִּי ,וַיִּמֹדֵד,

מַלְכֵי, וּבְאֵר, בְּשָׁלֹשׁ, הוֹסַף, שָׁוְא, יִתְפְּרוּ, אֲכַלְתֶּם,
זַעֲקִי, אֶכֹל, יִשְׁתַּדָּוֶה, וּלְשֵׁת, יְכַלְכְּלוּ, נִגְאֲלוּ, יֵאָסֵף,
נְבוּ, תִּמְשֹׁלְנָה, אֲדֹנִי, יֵשֵׁב, יִבְשֵׁת, אֵפוֹ, וְנִבְרְכָה,
שְׁמֶךָ, מִפְקָדִים, בְּצַלְמוֹ, מְקַלֲלוֹנִי.

§ 4. SYLLABLES.

1. Every syllable, and therefore every word,
must *begin* with a *consonant.* The conjunction
וְ = *and*, prefixed to *words*, whose first letter is
vowelless, or is a labial, בּ, מ, or פ, is the sole
exception to this rule; e.g. וּבְכֹל, וּמֶלֶךְ.

2. *Open* syllables are those which *end* in a
vowel sound; e.g. אֲנִי = ä-nee.

3. *Closed* or *shut* syllables are those which
end in a *consonant*; קָם.

4. *Long* vowels stand regularly in *open* syllables; תּוֹשִׁיבֵנִי.

5. *Short* vowels stand regularly in *shut* syllables; רַבְתֶּם.

6. An accent (§ 7, 3–§ 10) may reverse rules
4 and 5, and allow a *long* vowel to stand in a
shut syllable, or a *short* vowel in an *open* one;
e.g. יִרְאוּ = yĭ-r'oo, לָבְשָׁתָ = lä-väsh-tä.

7. In reading Hebrew, Vocal Sh'va may be
regarded as forming a sort of *open* syllable.
קָטְלָה = kät'-lä.

8. No syllable can contain more than a sin-

gle vowel. Two concurring vowels, as, e.g. in
our word "lion," never occur. See Rule 1.

EXERCISE XVI.

Divide each word in Exercises V., **X.**, **XII.**,
and **XV.** into its component syllables; give the
reason why each syllable is open or closed; and
also whether the syllable has its proper vowel,
together with the reason for it.

§ 5. DAGESH.

1. The dot in ת, פ, כ, ד, ג, ב is called the
DAGESH LENE, and serves to give to these
letters, called *aspirates* their hard sound, e.g.
פ = ph, or f, while פּ = p ; ת = th, while תּ = t.

2. A DAGESH FORTE is a simple dot which
may be placed in the bosom of any letter,
except the gutturals, viz. א, ה, ח, ע, and sometimes ר.

3. Its effect is to *double* the letter in which
it stands; e.g. קְטֹל = kăt-tāl, הֻגַּשׁ = hŭg-găsh.
Kăb-bā*th* must be written כַּבֵּד, not כְּבֵּד.

4. It is never found in a *vowelless final* letter
of a word, except in אַתְּ and נָתַתְּ.

5. It is very rarely found in the *first* letter
of a word.

6. When it occurs in an aspirate, ת, פ, כ, ד, ג, ב,
it not only *doubles* it, but also gives it the *hard*

sound; hence it is both *forte* and *lene;* e.g. דַּבֵּר,
the dot in ד is, of course, *lene*, but the dot in ב
makes the letter b, and also doubles it, so that
the word is pronounced dăb-bār.

7. The Dagesh in an aspirate can easily be
determined. If a vowel sound precede it, it
must be Dagesh *Forte;* if a silent Sh'va precede,
it is Dagesh *Lene;* e.g. כַּבֵּר, the Dagesh in פ
must be *forte.* In פִּי, יְפַתַּח, and קָטַלְתְּ the Dagesh is *lene.*

8. Double Vav (ו) has the same form as
Shoo-rĕk (וּ). When the preceding letter has
a vowel, ו = double v; otherwise it is ōō; e.g.
קִוָּם = kĭv-văm; but קוּם = koom.

9. In regard to syllabication, the letter in
which Dagesh Forte stands, *closes* one syllable,
and also *begins* another.

EXERCISE XVII.

Write in Hebrew characters the following
words.

Răbbeem, kăllăh, nĭttăch, nŭggăsh, kŭllee,
yĭttān, yĭksh'rĕnnee, bŏtteem, kăvvän, kŏlloo,
tsĭvväh, kĭyyām, măll'koo, mĭllā, g'mălleem,
t'fĭlläh, sŭbb'kō, mĭshsh'thā, y'shăddām, kŏlläh,
hĭthpăllā*t*, kă*tt*'läh, hĭmmälä*t*, shämmäh, tĭg-
g'shee, l'thĭttee, hĭnnĕnnee, hăssĕh, tĭttămmām,
vătt'fall'*tā*mo, kŏssoo, nĭttăttĕm, y'koonnĕnnoo,
yădd'kĭnnäh, hĭnnăbbeethä, vättĭssăbbee.

EXERCISE XVIII.

Divide each word into its component syllables. If Sh'va occurs, state why it is vocal
or silent. In the aspirates, state whether
Dagesh is lene or forte. And when they have
no Dagesh, give reason for its omission.

אֵפוֹ, חָיָב, עֵוֵת, חַלֹן, מְכַבֵּר, הֲבַקֹת, דִּבְּרוּ, גִּדַלְתִּי,

חָשְׁבָה, בְּדַבְּרִי, הֶפְבֵּס, קַרְדֻּמִּים, בְּרֻדִּים, וַיֵּדוּ, מְכַבֵּת,

כֻּפֵּת, כַּפְתֹּר, תִּפְבָּתִין, וַתִּפַּלְטֵמוֹ, מְדִי, מִדְכֶם, לְבוּ,

עֶזִּי, עַמְּכֶן, חַיֵּי, עֵיֵר, הִתְחַתֵּם, הֲדַבֵּר, כֻּלָּה, שַׁלַּח,

הֻכְּפָה, אֲעַמֵּד, אֲחַלֵּק, עֲמֹדְנָה, אֲטַמֵּעַ, אָמְךָ, מְמֶנּוּ,

אֶתֵּן, תַּחֲמֵּם, אֲוִיאֵל, אֶתֵּן, בַּצַּדִּיק, וַיְקַלֵּל, הַלֹּדֶה,

הַיֹּצֵא, הַזֶּה, הַמְנַשֶּׁה, אֲצַוֵּנוּ, כֻּלּוֹ, וַיְשֵׁנוּ, יַסְרֵנִי,

וַיִּפְתַּח, אֲמֹתוֹ, תִּתֹּךְ, שַׁבַּתּוֹ, נְכַבְּדֵי, לַדְנוּ, עָמְדִי,

הִתְפַּנְּסְתִּי, אֲקַבֵּץ, אָדַלֵּג, סֶקֶל, הַשַּׁבָּת, אֲדָמֶה, תְּשֻׁבֶךָ,

וְנִתְּהֶם, אֶתְּנֶנָּה, וַתִּפֹּל, וַיְטַלְלֵנוּ, הֻזַּכוּ, תֵּתֹשׁ, אֲקֹטֵר,

וְיִסְתַּבֵּל, אַטִּיג, הִצַּטַיֵּד, תַּנַּח, וַתִּתְּנָה, הִנַּבְּאוּ, הֲכֻּבֵּס,

תֻּסַּבִּי, הֶזְדֵּמְנָתוּן, תִּתְפָּל.

§ 6. PATTACH FURTIVE.

1. When Păttăch is written under either of
the gutturals ה, ח, or ע, standing at the end
of a word, it is called *furtive,* and is pro-

nounced *before* the guttural, instead of *after* it;
e.g. רוּחַ = rooăch, *not* roochă.

2. If a final vowelless letter follow the guttural pointed with Pattach, the Pattach in this case is also *furtive*, e.g. יַחְדְּ = yĭăchd, not yĭchăd. Forms of this sort are, however, comparatively rare.

(*a*) In order to pronounce the furtive Pattach, lay the stress of voice on the vowel preceding the guttural, and just touch the Pattach; somewhat as ă in the English words *trial, vial*, etc.

(*b*) "Analogous to this Pattach is our use of a *furtive* ĕ before r, after long ē, ī, ū; e.g. *here* (sounded hēᵉr), *fire* (fīᵉr), *pure* (pūᵉr)."

3. Pattach Furtive never forms an additional syllable; e.g. in רוּחַ, the syllable is *closed*, and the Pattach is simply wedged in between the ו and the ח.

EXERCISE XIX.

Examples for pronunciation.

כֹּחַ , רֵעַ , שָׁלוּחַ , גָּבוֹהַּ , שִׂיחַ , רֵיחַ , זְרַח , זְרוֹעַ ,

מִזְבֵּחַ , הִגִּיחַ , בּוּעַ , מָנוּחַ , נוּחַ , נֹּחַ , שֹׁמֵעַ , רוּעַ , גִּיחַ ,

הוֹדִיעַ , אֱלוֹהַּ , מַשְׁלִיחַ , מֵרַע , מָשֹׁחַ , מָשִׁיחַ , נֹבֵעַ ,

הִבִּיעַ , סָלֹחַ , אֶסְלוֹחַ , אֶפְתַּח , הַבְצַע , לִבְלוֹעַ , שָׁלַחְתְּ ,

הִגְנִיהַ .

5

§ 7. MAPPIK, MAKKEF, AND METHEG.

1. Măppĭk is a dot in a final ה, and serves
to show that it is a *consonant*, and not a mere
quiescent letter. Thus, in נֹגַהּ, ה is a consonant, and *closes* the syllable. In נָכָה, ה is a
quiescent, and merely prolongs the sound of
Kämĕts, while the syllable is *open*.

(*a*) Mappik cannot be confounded with Dagesh Forte, as the latter never occurs in gutturals or final letters.

2. Măkkĕf is a short horizontal bar (or hy-
phen) between two or more words; e.g. וַיְהִי־כֵן,
אֶת־כָּל־אֲשֶׁר־לוֹ, וְאִם־שָׁלֹשׁ־אֵלֶּה.

(*a*) When words are so connected, only the
last word has an accent, and the vowel in the
final syllable of the words preceding the Makkef is generally *short*.

3. Mĕthĕg is a small perpendicular line (|)
placed on the left of the vowel which stands in
the *second syllable before the tone*.

(*a*) Its usual position is by the vowel of the
antepenult. It can *never* occur in the *ult* or
penult; e.g. יַעֲמֹד, קְטָלוּ.

(*b*) Its force is that of a *secondary* accent,
analogous to that on the first syllable of our
words, *un`dertake´, an`ima´tion*.

(*c*) Polysyllabic words sometimes have two
or more Methegs; e.g. לִישׁוּעָתְךָ.

(*d*) A vowel with Metheg is usually *long*.

§ 8. KAMETS AND KAMETS-CHATOOF.

The surest guide for distinguishing between long ä and short ŏ (both represented by one sign, viz. ָ) is the *grammatical derivation* of a word.

For the beginner, the following rules will serve as a guide.

1. The sign ָ is short ŏ in a *closed unaccented* syllable.

2. The sign ָ is short ŏ in an *open* syllable only when followed by Kamets-Chatoof or by Chatef-Kamets.

3. Or, to express the rules in a different way, the sign ָ is short ŏ when followed by,

(1) Dagesh Forte: רָנִּי = rŏnnee ;

(2) Makkef: כָּל־ = kŏl ;

(3) Kamets-Chatoof: הָעָמְדִי = hŏʻŏmthee ;

(4) Chatef-Kamets: בָּחֳרִי = bŏchŏree ;

(5) Sh'va, without an intervening Metheg:
שָׁמְרָה = shŏmräh ; or,

(6) When it stands in a *closed final* syllable, with the accent on the *penult:*
וַיָּקָם = văyyäkŏm.

REM. 1. Case (5) is the only one which causes any perplexity. It is necessary to determine whether the syllable in which ָ stands is open or closed; to discover this we must know whether the Sh'va is vocal or silent. To tell whether the Sh'va is vocal or silent (unless it is followed by an undageshed aspirate, § 5, 1) we must know whether the preceding vowel is long or short, which is the very point in question.

But a general practical rule is to regard the $\overline{\ }$ when followed by $\overline{\cdot}$ without an intervening Metheg as short ŏ; e.g. קָטְלִי = kŏtlee, while קָטְלוּ = kät'loo.

A Dagesh Forte between the $\overline{\ }$ and the $\overline{\cdot}$ of course determines the sound as short ŏ, even though the $\overline{\ }$ be accompanied by Metheg; e.g. צָרַּךְ = tŏzz'kä.

REM. 2. Metheg also commonly stands by the Kamets-Chatoof when it is followed by another Kamets-Chatoof or by Chatef-Kamets (Cases 3 and 4). It is only when $\overline{\ }$ is followed by $\overline{\cdot}$ that the Metheg is of use to determine the sound as ä.

4. The first $\overline{\ }$ in the two anomalous words קָדָשִׁים and שָׁרָשִׁים is short ŏ. Pronounce kŏthä-sheem, shŏräsheem.

5. In all other cases besides those above mentioned, $\overline{\ }$ is long ä; viz. in *open* syllables, whether accented or not, whether they have a quiescent letter or not, and in *accented* syllables whether they be closed or followed by Dagesh Forte.

EXERCISE XX.

Write in Hebrew characters the following words.

NOTE.— Be careful to insert Metheg and silent Sh'va in their proper places.

Yŏktäl, bŏtneem, väyyä'rŏm, bŏttäkĕm, shäm, rŏnnoō, hŏᵎomäth, läk, gŏfreeth, y'chŏnkä, chŏn-nänoo, ℵŏznä, häläktä, häbbŏtteem, kŏl-d'vär, käl, kŏthkōth, shälōsh, kŏshräh, käsh'räh, yĭsh-mŏrkĕm, yäshŏv, pŏᵎŏlkĕm, yoomäth, väyyä-mŏth, ℵŏkläh, häggämäl kŏl-bäsär, kŏvᵎlō, kŏtŏvkä, shŏfk'kä, m'mŭlläk.

EXERCISE XXI.

Pronounce and write in English characters
the following words. Give the reason, in each
case why the sign ָ is long ā or short ŏ.

NOTE.—The accent is on the *last* syllable, except where otherwise marked by ʹ.

בָּתִּים ,יָשָׁב ,וַיֵּשֶׁב ,גָּלְמָה ,גָּלְמִי ,כֻּלָּמוּ ,חָק־

,קָרְאִי ,קָדְשִׁי ,שְׁפָטֵנִי ,הַבָּנִים ,הָיְתָה ,כָּל־ ,יָם ,בָּרְחִי

,גְּלִיַת ,מָצָא ,קָטְבְךָ ,סָב ,מֶלְכָה ,מַלְכָּה ,יָקְשָׁן ,בָּרְכוּ

,אָרְחֲךָ ,עָנוּ ,עָנְיִי ,שְׁפָטֵנִי ,לָמָּה ,אַהֲרֹן ,יְכָלְיָה ,יָד

,הָגִי ,דָּכָה ,דָּכִים ,דְּכִי ,כָּפְרוּ ,עָשְׂרָם ,גְּמַלֵּנִי ,מֵאֲחֻזִּים

,אָרְדָן ,אֲרָחוֹת ,יָקְטָן ,יָפִי ,יָפְיָפֶה ,הָפְשִׁי ,לֶחְלִי ,עָרְלָה

,יֵעָזָר־נָא ,עָשְׁקָה ,עָשְׁקָה ,אָרַךְ ,יְכָנְיָה ,הָנְתְּקוּ ,וַיִּנְּתְנוּ

,רָב־אָדָם ,רָב ,הֶחָלָה ,עָרְלָתוֹ ,אָרְנָן ,יָקְנְעָם ,בְּחַלְיוֹ

,מָשְׁלוּ ,מָשְׁלוּ ,אֶנְהַגְךָ ,נָדְדָה ,נָגֶךָ ,עָפְלֵיכֶם ,עֲפָאִים

,טָהֳרָה ,תּוֹרֹתְךָ ,לְחָק־עוֹלָם ,חֳמָרִים ,וַתִּכְתָּב־שָׁם

,כֻּתֳּנוֹת ,אָהֳלִי ,שֻׁדַּד ,כָּסוּ ,מְאָדָּם ,וְחֳלָיִים ,מָעֳמָד

,חָרְבַּת ,וָתָּחָם ,יָשְׁדֵּם ,אֲנַחְנוּ ,שָׁוְא ,חָכְמָה ,הָשְׁדָּבָה

,לָמָּה ,תֶּעָבְדֵם ,הָקִים ,מָוְתָה ,וּצְלָעֲקִי ,קָדְקֹדוּ ,קָסְבִּי

,מָרְטָה ,מֵאָסְכֶם ,בָּחֳרִים ,חֳלָיִים ,וַיָּלַט ,יַבָּשָׁה ,וַיָּעַף

,קִרְבְּכֶם ,קָטְנִי ,הָשְׁפוּת ,גָּדְל־ ,כָּנָף ,שָׁרֻךְ ,וַתָּהַס

,וַיָּצָם ,יָפְתִּי ,נָפְצָה ,אַבְחַנְךָ ,הָשַּׁמָּה ,פָּעֳלְכֶם ,קָטְנִי

וַיֵּשֶׁב, גֵּוִי, רָחְקָה, כָּלוּ, תְּאָרֵם, אָמְנָם, אֶעֱלֶה, סַלּוּהָ,

מָתְנַי, מֵאֵסוּ, וַחֲלִי, וְסַעֲדָה, דָּלְיוּ, דָּקַר, דְּלָתְךָ, הַגָּא,

יִמְשָׁל־בָּךְ, בָּחָרְתָּ, מֵהֲרָתָם.

§ 9. VAV AND YOTHE AS CONSONANTS.

1. (a) Whenever Vav is preceded by any
other vowel than Shoorĕk, Kĭbboots, or Chō-
lĕm; or whenever Yothe is preceded by any
other vowel than Cheerĕk, Tsārā, or Sĕgŏl; or
(b) whenever they receive Dagesh Forte; or
(c) have a vowel or vocal Sh'va; or (d) stand
at the beginning of a word, they are treated as
consonants, viz. v or y; thus וַ = äv, as in וָו ;
וַ = ăv, as in גַּו; וָ = āv, as in גֵּו; וֶ = ĕv, as
in שֶׁלֶו; וִ = ĭv, as in צִו; יִי (like וִ) = ăv, as
in בָּנָיו, pronounced bänäv.

Thus יַ or יִ = aī,* as in *aisle* (not like ai in
pail), צָרַי = tsāraī; וֹי = ōy, sounded not like
oy in *boy*, but more like oee, e.g. גוֹי = goee;
וִי = ooy, like uoy in *buoy*, i.e. ooee; e.g. גָּלוּי =
gälooee.

As the forms in which Yothe takes Dagesh
Forte cause the beginner some perplexity, the
pronunciation of some of these forms is here
given.

---

* Whenever aī occurs in this section, it is always to be so
pronounced.

יִ֖ =	eeyee,	e.g.	צִיִּים =	tsee-yeem.
יָה֖ =	ecyäh,		צִיָה =	tsee-yüh.
יוֹ֖ =	eeyō,		צִיוֹן =	tsee-yōn.
יֶה֖ =	eeyĕh,		צִיֶה =	tsee-yĕh.
יוּ֖ =	eeyoo,		צִיּוּן =	tsee-yoon.
יִ֖ =	aīyee,		חַיִּים =	chaī-yeem.
יִַ֖ =	aīyaī,		חַיַּי =	chaī-yaī.
יָה֖ =	aīyäh,		הַיָה =	chaī-yäh.
יוֹ֖ =	aīyō,		חַיּוֹת =	chaī-yōth.
יוֹ֖ =	ooyō,		מַלְכֻיּוֹת =	malkoo-yōth.

2. (a) When the *full* form for Cholem (וֹ) has a vowel *under* it, it is to be read ōv, and not simple ō ; e.g. לוֶֹה = lōväh, not lō-äh.

(b) If the preceding letter has a vowel or vocal Sh'va, וֹ is to be read vō ; e.g. עָוֹן = ȝävōn, not ȝäōn, for two vowels can never thus concur.

EXERCISE XXII.

Pronounce the following words.

State whether וֹ or יֹ, whenever either of them occurs, is a consonant or a quiescent, and why ?

וַיִּמְשֹׁל, עִבְרִיִּים, אִיִּים, אִיִּי, אַיֶּה, אַיָּה, אֵיָה, אֵיָה, אַיֵּה, אִיּוּ,

אִיּוֹב, בַּיְקֹשֹׁר, וַיְלַמֵּד, עָלָיו, דָּיָה, חַיַּת, סוּסִי, סוּתָיו,

יֶחֱזָיָה, בַּו, כַּוְיָה, פִּיּוֹן, כִּיר, וַיִּלְוֶה, הָיָה, וַיִּזְמֹר,

מִיָּמִין, נְוִית, נָבְרִיּוֹת, מָנוּי, כָּסוּי, וַיַּאֲסַר, סִינָן, עֲלַי,

יֵרַשֵׁב, עֵוֵּר, נְקִים, שָׂסוּי, שַׁוָּה, בּוֹכִיָה, סְכִיִּים, עִיָה,

סִיּוֹן, עַיּוּת, קַיִם, וַיְּצָמַח, צַוָּארָיו, פִּיּוֹת פִּיָה, עַתַּי,

עָשׂוּי, וַיַּעַשׂ, עָשָׂה, עִיִּים, מַחֲלֻוִי, קָנוּ, תְּפַיִם, וַיֹּאמֶר,

סָלֵוּ, שָׁלֵוּ, שְׂכִיָּה, דַּי, שַׂי, וַיִּרְכַּב, רַגְלָיו, רַגְלֵי, פִּיו,

הוִי, וַיִּרְאוּ, וִיְהִי, אוֹי, צִפּוֹי, אֲדֹנָי, שַׂדַּי, הוֹרִי, הוֹזִי,

נְקֹים, חֲנִיֹּות, הֶחֱבִּיו, גַּי, בְּדַי, תֵּמַי, חֲבִי, עֲמִי, לִחְיָי,

פִּילָיו, עֵינָיו, יוֹנָיו, יָדָיו, שִׁירָיו, חַיָּתוֹ, אַרְיֵךְ, דְּרָכַי,

הַיּוֹם, פָּנָיו, קָם, וַיּוֹשֶׁב, וַיִּיצֶר, וַיַּשְׂט, וַיִּקְבְּצוּ, וַיִּקְרָא,

אָחִיו, בָּנָיו, לָוֶה, קֹוֵי, שֹׁוֶה, גֹּוֶךְ, גֹּוֵיךְ, דַּוָּי, קֹוֶה,

דֹּוד, קֹוֵי, הֹוֶה, גֹּוֵעַ, קֹוֵו, גֹּוֵעַ, הֹוֶה, קֹוֶה, נָוֹת, הֹוֹת,

יְהֹוָה, מִצְוֹתָיו, קַצְוֹתָיו, כְּנֹותוֹ, עֵדֹות, וּמְשֻׁוֹנֹתֵיהֶם.

§ 10. ACCENT.

1. In addition to the vowel points, Dagesh, Mappik, Metheg, etc., Hebrew words in the Bible are furnished with accents, which indicate either (1) the tone-syllable, or (2) the syntactical relation which each word of a sentence bears to the rest.

2. The following is a list of the various forms of the accents, with their names.

1.	Sĭllook.	10.	Păshtä.	19.	P'seek.
2.	Athnäch.	11.	Zărkä.	20.	Moonäch.
3.	Mĕrkä.	12.	Y'theev.	21.	Kădmä.
4.	Tĭfchäh.	13.	Gĕrĕsh.	22.	Double Mĕrkä.
5.	Zäkĕf Kätōn.	14.	Double Gĕrĕsh.	23.	Mähpäk.
6.	Zäkĕf Gäthōl.	15.	Great T'lishä.	24.	Shälshĕlĕth.
7.	Sĕghōltä.	16.	Little T'lishä.	25.	Därgä.
8.	T'veer.	17.	Kärnä Färä.	26.	Y'räch.
9.	R'veeä.	18.	Päzĕr.		

3. These forms, except the first two, need not now be learnt. It suffices to remember, that if there be but *one* accent on a word, it generally denotes the *tone* syllable, i.e. the syllable upon which *the stress of voice is to be laid*. If there be two *different* accents on a word, the *second* one marks the tone; but if both accents be *alike*, then the *first* marks it.

4. Monosyllables, unless followed by Metheg, have the tone. In most words, the *ultimate* syllable has the tone; e.g. זָכַן, מוֹעֵד. In words that have ַ in the ult, the tone is on the *penult;* e.g. מֶלֶךְ = mĕ'lĕk. The tone is also on the *penult* in words preceded by וַ; וַיָּשָׁב = văyyä'shōv.

5. The tone can only be on the *ult* or *penult*, never on the antepenult.

6. The mark : called Sōf-P'sook always separates the verses, and takes the place of our period. The Athnăch ‸ stands about the middle of the verse, and divides it into two clauses. [In poetry the Merka serves the same purpose].

7. The syllables that have Sillook (which occurs only under the *last* word of a verse, immediately preceding Sōf-P'sook) or Athnach are said to be "in pause." Hence the vowel of such syllables is usually lengthened; e.g. רְכַב in pause becomes רְכָב.

8. The Sillook ַ can never be confounded with Metheg ָ, as the former stands only under

the *last* word of a verse, and then *always under
the tone-syllable*, while Metheg *never* stands under the tone-syllable.

State upon which syllable the stress of voice
is to be laid in each word of the first chapter
of Genesis; and for what reasons.

§ 11. K'REE AND K'THEE*V*.

1. K'ree means *marginal reading*. K'thee*v*
means *the text*. A star * or circle ° over a word
in the text directs the attention to the foot of
the page.

2. The vowels under the consonants of the
word in the text belong to the *consonants in the
margin*, not to the word in the text. Thus, in
Jer. xlii. 6, the text has אֲנוּ, the margin has
אנחנו, therefore אֲנוּ is to be pronounced אֲנַחְנוּ.
The proper vowels for אנו would be אָנוּ; cf.
1 Sam. v. 6; 2 Kings xvii. 16.

3. If a word in the text has no vowels, it is
regarded as superfluous; e.g. Jer. li. 3.

· 4. When vowels alone are found in the
text, the consonants to which they belong are
printed in the margin. Thus, in Judges xx.
13, ֵ*ְ stands in the text; in the margin we
have בְּנֵי; cf. 2 Sam. viii. 3; 2 Kings xix. 31, 37.

5. There are a few standing K'rees which are

unnoticed in the margin ; e.g. הָיו [in the Penta-
teuch] should always be pronounced Hee, not
Heev. יִשָּׂשכָר = yĭssäkär. The Jews super-
stitiously refrain from pronouncing the Divine
Name יהוה, but always pronounce it ᵃthōnaī,
whose vowels it is pointed with. However, *we*
usually read it as it is pointed, and pronounce
it Jehovah. If אֲדֹנָי precede it, it is pointed
יֱהוִֹה, which a Jew would pronounce ᵉlōheem.

DIRECTIONS TO THE STUDENT.

Note. — The following chapters are . inserted for practice in reading the text, and in applying the foregoing rules. These "directions" will indicate to the student the several points to which attention should be paid.

1. Practice reading these chapters *aloud*, until they can be read with accuracy and ease.

2. Divide each word into its component syllables, and give the rule for each syllable. § 4.

3. Give rule for the use of each vowel that occurs. § 4, 4–7.

4. Distinguish the vocal and silent Sh'vas.

5. In case of each Sh'va, state why it is vocal or silent. § 3.

6. Distinguish Dagesh Lene from Dagesh Forte. § 5.

7. Note *final* letters and *dilated* letters.

8. Note the quiescent letters. § 2, 3–4.

9. Select the words in which Mappik occurs.

10. Select the words in which Pattach Furtive occurs. § 6.

11. Find instances in which Cholem coincides with the diacritical point of ש. § 2, 5.

12. Find the words in which Kamets-Chatoof occurs. § 8.

GENESIS.

בראשית·

CAPUT I. א

בְּרֵאשִׁית בָּרָא אֱלֹהִים אֵת הַשָּׁמַיִם וְאֵת הָאָרֶץ: וְהָאָרֶץ ‏‏‎ א‎2

הָיְתָה תֹהוּ וָבֹהוּ וְחֹשֶׁךְ עַל־פְּנֵי תְהוֹם וְרוּחַ אֱלֹהִים

מְרַחֶפֶת עַל־פְּנֵי הַמָּיִם: וַיֹּאמֶר אֱלֹהִים יְהִי אוֹר וַיְהִי־ ‏‎ 3

אוֹר: וַיַּרְא אֱלֹהִים אֶת־הָאוֹר כִּי־טוֹב וַיַּבְדֵּל אֱלֹהִים בֵּין ‏‎ 4

הָאוֹר וּבֵין הַחֹשֶׁךְ: וַיִּקְרָא אֱלֹהִים ׀ לָאוֹר יוֹם וְלַחֹשֶׁךְ ‏‎ ה

קָרָא לָיְלָה וַיְהִי־עֶרֶב וַיְהִי־בֹקֶר יוֹם אֶחָד: ‏‎ פ

וַיֹּאמֶר אֱלֹהִים יְהִי רָקִיעַ בְּתוֹךְ הַמָּיִם וִיהִי מַבְדִּיל בֵּין ‏‎ 6

מַיִם לָמָיִם: וַיַּעַשׂ אֱלֹהִים אֶת־הָרָקִיעַ וַיַּבְדֵּל בֵּין הַמַּיִם ‏‎ 7

אֲשֶׁר מִתַּחַת לָרָקִיעַ וּבֵין הַמַּיִם אֲשֶׁר מֵעַל לָרָקִיעַ וַיְהִי־

כֵן: וַיִּקְרָא אֱלֹהִים לָרָקִיעַ שָׁמָיִם וַיְהִי־עֶרֶב וַיְהִי־בֹקֶר ‏‎ 8

יוֹם שֵׁנִי: ‏‎ פ ‏‎ וַיֹּאמֶר אֱלֹהִים יִקָּווּ הַמַּיִם מִתַּחַת ‏‎ 9

הַשָּׁמַיִם אֶל־מָקוֹם אֶחָד וְתֵרָאֶה הַיַּבָּשָׁה וַיְהִי־כֵן:

וַיִּקְרָא אֱלֹהִים ׀ לַיַּבָּשָׁה אֶרֶץ וּלְמִקְוֵה הַמַּיִם קָרָא יַמִּים ‏‎ י

11 וַיַּ֥רְא אֱלֹהִ֖ים כִּי־ט֑וֹב׃ וַיֹּ֣אמֶר אֱלֹהִ֗ים תַּֽדְשֵׁ֤א הָאָ֨רֶץ֙
דֶּ֗שֶׁא עֵ֚שֶׂב מַזְרִ֣יעַ זֶ֔רַע עֵ֣ץ פְּרִ֞י עֹ֤שֶׂה פְּרִי֙ לְמִינ֔וֹ אֲשֶׁ֥ר

12 זַרְעוֹ־ב֖וֹ עַל־הָאָ֑רֶץ וַֽיְהִי־כֵֽן׃ וַתּוֹצֵ֨א הָאָ֜רֶץ דֶּ֠שֶׁא עֵ֣שֶׂב
מַזְרִ֤יעַ זֶ֨רַע֙ לְמִינֵ֔הוּ וְעֵ֧ץ עֹֽשֶׂה־פְּרִ֛י אֲשֶׁ֥ר זַרְעוֹ־ב֖וֹ לְמִינֵ֑הוּ

13 וַיַּ֥רְא אֱלֹהִ֖ים כִּי־ט֑וֹב׃ וַֽיְהִי־עֶ֥רֶב וַֽיְהִי־בֹ֖קֶר י֥וֹם שְׁלִישִֽׁי׃

14 פ   וַיֹּ֣אמֶר אֱלֹהִ֗ים יְהִ֤י מְאֹרֹת֙ בִּרְקִ֣יעַ הַשָּׁמַ֔יִם
לְהַבְדִּ֕יל בֵּ֥ין הַיּ֖וֹם וּבֵ֣ין הַלָּ֑יְלָה וְהָי֤וּ לְאֹתֹת֙ וּלְמ֣וֹעֲדִ֔ים

טו וּלְיָמִ֖ים וְשָׁנִֽים׃ וְהָי֤וּ לִמְאוֹרֹת֙ בִּרְקִ֣יעַ הַשָּׁמַ֔יִם לְהָאִ֖יר

16 עַל־הָאָ֑רֶץ וַֽיְהִי־כֵֽן׃ וַיַּ֣עַשׂ אֱלֹהִ֔ים אֶת־שְׁנֵ֥י הַמְּאֹרֹ֖ת
הַגְּדֹלִ֑ים אֶת־הַמָּא֤וֹר הַגָּדֹל֙ לְמֶמְשֶׁ֣לֶת הַיּ֔וֹם וְאֶת־הַמָּא֤וֹר

17 הַקָּטֹן֙ לְמֶמְשֶׁ֣לֶת הַלַּ֔יְלָה וְאֵ֖ת הַכּֽוֹכָבִֽים׃ וַיִּתֵּ֥ן אֹתָ֛ם

18 אֱלֹהִ֖ים בִּרְקִ֣יעַ הַשָּׁמָ֑יִם לְהָאִ֖יר עַל־הָאָֽרֶץ׃ וְלִמְשֹׁל֙
בַּיּ֣וֹם וּבַלַּ֔יְלָה וּֽלֲהַבְדִּ֔יל בֵּ֥ין הָא֖וֹר וּבֵ֣ין הַחֹ֑שֶׁךְ וַיַּ֥רְא

19 אֱלֹהִ֖ים כִּי־ט֑וֹב׃ וַֽיְהִי־עֶ֥רֶב וַֽיְהִי־בֹ֖קֶר י֥וֹם רְבִיעִֽי׃ פ

כ   וַיֹּ֣אמֶר אֱלֹהִ֔ים יִשְׁרְצ֣וּ הַמַּ֔יִם שֶׁ֖רֶץ נֶ֣פֶשׁ חַיָּ֑ה

21 וְעוֹף֙ יְעוֹפֵ֣ף עַל־הָאָ֔רֶץ עַל־פְּנֵ֖י רְקִ֣יעַ הַשָּׁמָֽיִם׃ וַיִּבְרָ֣א
אֱלֹהִ֔ים אֶת־הַתַּנִּינִ֖ם הַגְּדֹלִ֑ים וְאֵ֣ת כָּל־נֶ֣פֶשׁ הַֽחַיָּ֣ה ׀
הָֽרֹמֶ֡שֶׂת אֲשֶׁר֩ שָׁרְצ֨וּ הַמַּ֜יִם לְמִֽינֵהֶ֗ם וְאֵ֤ת כָּל־ע֣וֹף כָּנָ֔ף

22 לְמִינֵהוּ וַיַּרְא אֱלֹהִים כִּי־טֽוֹב: וַיְבָ֣רֶךְ אֹתָ֥ם אֱלֹהִים לֵאמֹ֑ר
פְּר֣וּ וּרְב֗וּ וּמִלְא֤וּ אֶת־הַמַּ֨יִם֙ בַּיַּמִּ֔ים וְהָע֖וֹף יִ֥רֶב בָּאָֽרֶץ:

23
24 וַֽיְהִי־עֶ֥רֶב וַֽיְהִי־בֹ֖קֶר י֥וֹם חֲמִישִֽׁי: פ וַיֹּ֣אמֶר
אֱלֹהִ֗ים תּוֹצֵ֤א הָאָ֨רֶץ֙ נֶ֣פֶשׁ חַיָּה֙ לְמִינָ֔הּ בְּהֵמָ֥ה וָרֶ֛מֶשׂ

כה וְחַֽיְתוֹ־אֶ֖רֶץ לְמִינָ֑הּ וַֽיְהִי־כֵֽן: וַיַּ֣עַשׂ אֱלֹהִים֮ אֶת־חַיַּ֣ת
הָאָ֜רֶץ לְמִינָ֗הּ וְאֶת־הַבְּהֵמָה֙ לְמִינָ֔הּ וְאֵ֛ת כָּל־רֶ֥מֶשׂ

26 הָֽאֲדָמָ֖ה לְמִינֵ֑הוּ וַיַּ֥רְא אֱלֹהִ֖ים כִּי־טֽוֹב: וַיֹּ֣אמֶר אֱלֹהִ֔ים
נַֽעֲשֶׂ֥ה אָדָ֛ם בְּצַלְמֵ֖נוּ כִּדְמוּתֵ֑נוּ וְיִרְדּוּ֩ בִדְגַ֨ת הַיָּ֜ם וּבְע֣וֹף
הַשָּׁמַ֗יִם וּבַבְּהֵמָה֙ וּבְכָל־הָאָ֔רֶץ וּבְכָל־הָרֶ֖מֶשׂ הָֽרֹמֵ֥שׂ

27 עַל־הָאָֽרֶץ: וַיִּבְרָ֨א אֱלֹהִ֤ים ׀ אֶת־הָֽאָדָם֙ בְּצַלְמ֔וֹ בְּצֶ֥לֶם
28 אֱלֹהִ֖ים בָּרָ֣א אֹת֑וֹ זָכָ֥ר וּנְקֵבָ֖ה בָּרָ֥א אֹתָֽם: וַיְבָ֣רֶךְ אֹתָם֮
אֱלֹהִים֒ וַיֹּ֨אמֶר לָהֶ֜ם אֱלֹהִ֗ים פְּר֥וּ וּרְב֛וּ וּמִלְא֥וּ אֶת־הָאָ֖רֶץ
וְכִבְשֻׁ֑הָ וּרְד֞וּ בִּדְגַ֤ת הַיָּם֙ וּבְע֣וֹף הַשָּׁמַ֔יִם וּבְכָל־חַיָּ֖ה

29 הָֽרֹמֶ֥שֶׂת עַל־הָאָֽרֶץ: וַיֹּ֣אמֶר אֱלֹהִ֗ים הִנֵּה֩ נָתַ֨תִּי לָכֶ֜ם
אֶת־כָּל־עֵ֣שֶׂב ׀ זֹרֵ֣עַ זֶ֗רַע אֲשֶׁר֙ עַל־פְּנֵ֣י כָל־הָאָ֔רֶץ וְאֶת־כָּל־
הָעֵ֛ץ אֲשֶׁר־בּ֥וֹ פְרִי־עֵ֖ץ זֹרֵ֣עַ זָ֑רַע לָכֶ֥ם יִֽהְיֶ֖ה לְאָכְלָֽה:

ל וּֽלְכָל־חַיַּ֣ת הָ֠אָרֶץ וּלְכָל־ע֨וֹף הַשָּׁמַ֜יִם וּלְכֹ֣ל ׀ רוֹמֵ֣שׂ עַל־
הָאָ֗רֶץ אֲשֶׁר־בּוֹ֙ נֶ֣פֶשׁ חַיָּ֔ה אֶת־כָּל־יֶ֥רֶק עֵ֖שֶׂב לְאָכְלָ֑ה

31 וַיְהִי־כֵן: וַיַּרְא אֱלֹהִים אֶת־כָּל־אֲשֶׁר עָשָׂה וְהִנֵּה־טוֹב
מְאֹד וַיְהִי־עֶרֶב וַיְהִי־בֹקֶר יוֹם הַשִּׁשִּׁי: פ

ב

CAP. II. ב

2 וַיְכֻלּוּ הַשָּׁמַיִם וְהָאָרֶץ וְכָל־צְבָאָם: וַיְכַל אֱלֹהִים בַּיּוֹם
הַשְּׁבִיעִי מְלַאכְתּוֹ אֲשֶׁר עָשָׂה וַיִּשְׁבֹּת בַּיּוֹם הַשְּׁבִיעִי
3 מִכָּל־מְלַאכְתּוֹ אֲשֶׁר עָשָׂה: וַיְבָרֶךְ אֱלֹהִים אֶת־יוֹם
הַשְּׁבִיעִי וַיְקַדֵּשׁ אֹתוֹ כִּי בוֹ שָׁבַת מִכָּל־מְלַאכְתּוֹ אֲשֶׁר־
4 בָּרָא אֱלֹהִים לַעֲשׂוֹת: פ   אֵלֶּה תוֹלְדוֹת הַשָּׁמַיִם
וְהָאָרֶץ בְּהִבָּרְאָם בְּיוֹם עֲשׂוֹת יְהֹוָה אֱלֹהִים אֶרֶץ
5 וְשָׁמָיִם: וְכֹל ׀ שִׂיחַ הַשָּׂדֶה טֶרֶם יִהְיֶה בָאָרֶץ וְכָל־
עֵשֶׂב הַשָּׂדֶה טֶרֶם יִצְמָח כִּי לֹא הִמְטִיר יְהֹוָה אֱלֹהִים
6 עַל־הָאָרֶץ וְאָדָם אַיִן לַעֲבֹד אֶת־הָאֲדָמָה: וְאֵד יַעֲלֶה
7 מִן־הָאָרֶץ וְהִשְׁקָה אֶת־כָּל־פְּנֵי הָאֲדָמָה: וַיִּיצֶר יְהֹוָה
אֱלֹהִים אֶת־הָאָדָם עָפָר מִן־הָאֲדָמָה וַיִּפַּח בְּאַפָּיו נִשְׁמַת
8 חַיִּים וַיְהִי הָאָדָם לְנֶפֶשׁ חַיָּה: וַיִּטַּע יְהֹוָה אֱלֹהִים
9 גַּן־בְּעֵדֶן מִקֶּדֶם וַיָּשֶׂם שָׁם אֶת־הָאָדָם אֲשֶׁר יָצָר: וַיַּצְמַח
יְהֹוָה אֱלֹהִים מִן־הָאֲדָמָה כָּל־עֵץ נֶחְמָד לְמַרְאֶה וְטוֹב
לְמַאֲכָל וְעֵץ הַחַיִּים בְּתוֹךְ הַגָּן וְעֵץ הַדַּעַת טוֹב וָרָע:

‏וְנָהָר יֹצֵא מֵעֵדֶן לְהַשְׁקוֹת אֶת־הַגָּן וּמִשָּׁם יִפָּרֵד וְהָיָה‎ ‏י‎

‏לְאַרְבָּעָה רָאשִׁים: שֵׁם הָאֶחָד פִּישׁוֹן הוּא הַסֹּבֵב‎ 11

‏אֵת כָּל־אֶרֶץ הַחֲוִילָה אֲשֶׁר־שָׁם הַזָּהָב: וּזֲהַב הָאָרֶץ‎ 12

‏הַהִוא טוֹב שָׁם הַבְּדֹלַח וְאֶבֶן הַשֹּׁהַם: וְשֵׁם־הַנָּהָר‎ 13

‏הַשֵּׁנִי גִּיחוֹן הוּא הַסּוֹבֵב אֵת כָּל־אֶרֶץ כּוּשׁ: וְשֵׁם־הַנָּהָר‎ 14

‏הַשְּׁלִישִׁי חִדֶּקֶל הוּא הַהֹלֵךְ קִדְמַת אַשּׁוּר וְהַנָּהָר‎

‏הָרְבִיעִי הוּא פְרָת: וַיִּקַּח יְהֹוָה אֱלֹהִים אֶת־הָאָדָם‎ ‏טו‎

‏וַיַּנִּחֵהוּ בְגַן־עֵדֶן לְעָבְדָהּ וּלְשָׁמְרָהּ: וַיְצַו יְהֹוָה אֱלֹהִים‎ 16

‏עַל־הָאָדָם לֵאמֹר מִכֹּל עֵץ־הַגָּן אָכֹל תֹּאכֵל: וּמֵעֵץ הַדַּעַת‎ 17

‏טוֹב וָרָע לֹא תֹאכַל מִמֶּנּוּ כִּי בְּיוֹם אֲכָלְךָ מִמֶּנּוּ מוֹת‎

‏תָּמוּת: וַיֹּאמֶר יְהֹוָה אֱלֹהִים לֹא־טוֹב הֱיוֹת הָאָדָם‎ 18

‏לְבַדּוֹ אֶעֱשֶׂה־לּוֹ עֵזֶר כְּנֶגְדּוֹ: וַיִּצֶר יְהֹוָה אֱלֹהִים מִן־‎ 19

‏הָאֲדָמָה כָּל־חַיַּת הַשָּׂדֶה וְאֵת כָּל־עוֹף הַשָּׁמַיִם וַיָּבֵא‎

‏אֶל־הָאָדָם לִרְאוֹת מַה־יִּקְרָא־לוֹ וְכֹל אֲשֶׁר יִקְרָא־לוֹ הָאָדָם‎

‏נֶפֶשׁ חַיָּה הוּא שְׁמוֹ: וַיִּקְרָא הָאָדָם שֵׁמוֹת לְכָל־‎ ‏כ‎

‏הַבְּהֵמָה וּלְעוֹף הַשָּׁמַיִם וּלְכֹל חַיַּת הַשָּׂדֶה וּלְאָדָם‎

‏לֹא־מָצָא עֵזֶר כְּנֶגְדּוֹ: וַיַּפֵּל יְהֹוָה אֱלֹהִים ׀ תַּרְדֵּמָה‎ 21

‏עַל־הָאָדָם וַיִּישָׁן וַיִּקַּח אַחַת מִצַּלְעֹתָיו וַיִּסְגֹּר בָּשָׂר‎

‏22 תַּחְתֶּנָּה: וַיִּבֶן יְהוָֹה אֱלֹהִים ׀ אֶת־הַצֵּלָע אֲשֶׁר־לָקַח מִן־‏

‏23 הָאָדָם לְאִשָּׁה וַיְבִאֶהָ אֶל־הָאָדָם: וַיֹּאמֶר הָאָדָם זֹאת‏

‏הַפַּעַם עֶצֶם מֵעֲצָמַי וּבָשָׂר מִבְּשָׂרִי לְזֹאת יִקָּרֵא אִשָּׁה‏

‏24 כִּי מֵאִישׁ לֻקֳחָה־זֹּאת: עַל־כֵּן יַעֲזָב־אִישׁ אֶת־אָבִיו וְאֶת־‏

‏25 אִמּוֹ וְדָבַק בְּאִשְׁתּוֹ וְהָיוּ לְבָשָׂר אֶחָד: וַיִּהְיוּ שְׁנֵיהֶם‏

‏עֲרוּמִּים הָאָדָם וְאִשְׁתּוֹ וְלֹא יִתְבֹּשָׁשׁוּ:‏

‏ג‏

Cap. III. ‏ג‏

‏1 וְהַנָּחָשׁ הָיָה עָרוּם מִכֹּל חַיַּת הַשָּׂדֶה אֲשֶׁר עָשָׂה יְהוָֹה‏

‏אֱלֹהִים וַיֹּאמֶר אֶל־הָאִשָּׁה אַף כִּי־אָמַר אֱלֹהִים לֹא‏

‏2 תֹאכְלוּ מִכֹּל עֵץ הַגָּן: וַתֹּאמֶר הָאִשָּׁה אֶל־הַנָּחָשׁ מִפְּרִי‏

‏3 עֵץ־הַגָּן נֹאכֵל: וּמִפְּרִי הָעֵץ אֲשֶׁר בְּתוֹךְ־הַגָּן אָמַר‏

‏4 אֱלֹהִים לֹא תֹאכְלוּ מִמֶּנּוּ וְלֹא תִגְּעוּ בּוֹ פֶּן־תְּמֻתוּן: וַיֹּאמֶר‏

‏5 הַנָּחָשׁ אֶל־הָאִשָּׁה לֹא־מוֹת תְּמֻתוּן: כִּי יֹדֵעַ אֱלֹהִים כִּי‏

‏בְּיוֹם אֲכָלְכֶם מִמֶּנּוּ וְנִפְקְחוּ עֵינֵיכֶם וִהְיִיתֶם כֵּאלֹהִים‏

‏6 יֹדְעֵי טוֹב וָרָע: וַתֵּרֶא הָאִשָּׁה כִּי טוֹב הָעֵץ לְמַאֲכָל וְכִי‏

‏תַאֲוָה־הוּא לָעֵינַיִם וְנֶחְמָד הָעֵץ לְהַשְׂכִּיל וַתִּקַּח מִפִּרְיוֹ‏

‏7 וַתֹּאכַל וַתִּתֵּן גַּם־לְאִישָׁהּ עִמָּהּ וַיֹּאכַל: וַתִּפָּקַחְנָה עֵינֵי‏

‏שְׁנֵיהֶם וַיֵּדְעוּ כִּי עֵירֻמִּם הֵם וַיִּתְפְּרוּ עֲלֵה תְאֵנָה וַיַּעֲשׂוּ‏

‏לָהֶם חֲגֹרֹת: וַיִּשְׁמְעוּ אֶת־קוֹל יְהוָֹה אֱלֹהִים מִתְהַלֵּךְ‎ 8

‏בַּגָּן לְרוּחַ הַיּוֹם וַיִּתְחַבֵּא הָאָדָם וְאִשְׁתּוֹ מִפְּנֵי יְהוָֹה‎

‏אֱלֹהִים בְּתוֹךְ עֵץ הַגָּן: וַיִּקְרָא יְהוָֹה אֱלֹהִים אֶל־הָאָדָם‎ 9

‏וַיֹּאמֶר לוֹ אַיֶּךָּה: וַיֹּאמֶר אֶת־קֹלְךָ שָׁמַעְתִּי בַגָּן וָאִירָא‎ י

‏כִּי־עֵירֹם אָנֹכִי וָאֵחָבֵא: וַיֹּאמֶר מִי הִגִּיד לְךָ כִּי עֵירֹם‎ 11

‏אָתָּה הֲמִן־הָעֵץ אֲשֶׁר צִוִּיתִיךָ לְבִלְתִּי אֲכָל־מִמֶּנּוּ אָכָלְתָּ:‎

‏וַיֹּאמֶר הָאָדָם הָאִשָּׁה אֲשֶׁר נָתַתָּה עִמָּדִי הִוא נָתְנָה־לִי‎ 12

‏מִן־הָעֵץ וָאֹכֵל: וַיֹּאמֶר יְהוָֹה אֱלֹהִים לָאִשָּׁה מַה־זֹּאת‎ 13

‏עָשִׂית וַתֹּאמֶר הָאִשָּׁה הַנָּחָשׁ הִשִּׁיאַנִי וָאֹכֵל: וַיֹּאמֶר‎ 14

‏יְהוָֹה אֱלֹהִים ׀ אֶל־הַנָּחָשׁ כִּי עָשִׂיתָ זֹּאת אָרוּר אַתָּה‎

‏מִכָּל־הַבְּהֵמָה וּמִכֹּל חַיַּת הַשָּׂדֶה עַל־גְּחֹנְךָ תֵלֵךְ וְעָפָר‎

‏תֹּאכַל כָּל־יְמֵי חַיֶּיךָ: וְאֵיבָה ׀ אָשִׁית בֵּינְךָ וּבֵין הָאִשָּׁה‎ טו

‏וּבֵין זַרְעֲךָ וּבֵין זַרְעָהּ הוּא יְשׁוּפְךָ רֹאשׁ וְאַתָּה תְּשׁוּפֶנּוּ‎

‏עָקֵב: ס אֶל־הָאִשָּׁה אָמַר הַרְבָּה אַרְבֶּה עִצְּבוֹנֵךְ‎ 16

‏וְהֵרֹנֵךְ בְּעֶצֶב תֵּלְדִי בָנִים וְאֶל־אִישֵׁךְ תְּשׁוּקָתֵךְ וְהוּא‎

‏יִמְשָׁל־בָּךְ: ס וּלְאָדָם אָמַר כִּי שָׁמַעְתָּ לְקוֹל אִשְׁתֶּךָ‎ 17

‏וַתֹּאכַל מִן־הָעֵץ אֲשֶׁר צִוִּיתִיךָ לֵאמֹר לֹא תֹאכַל מִמֶּנּוּ‎

‏אֲרוּרָה הָאֲדָמָה בַּעֲבוּרֶךָ בְּעִצָּבוֹן תֹּאכֲלֶנָּה כֹּל יְמֵי‎

18 ‏חַיֶּיךָ: וְקוֹץ וְדַרְדַּר תַּצְמִיחַ לָךְ וְאָכַלְתָּ אֶת־עֵשֶׂב‏

19 ‏הַשָּׂדֶה: בְּזֵעַת אַפֶּיךָ תֹּאכַל לֶחֶם עַד שׁוּבְךָ אֶל־‏

‏הָאֲדָמָה כִּי מִמֶּנָּה לֻקָּחְתָּ כִּי־עָפָר אַתָּה וְאֶל־עָפָר‏

‏תָּשׁוּב: וַיִּקְרָא הָאָדָם שֵׁם אִשְׁתּוֹ חַוָּה כִּי הִוא הָיְתָה‏ ‏כ‏

21 ‏אֵם כָּל־חָי: וַיַּעַשׂ יְהֹוָה אֱלֹהִים לְאָדָם וּלְאִשְׁתּוֹ כָּתְנוֹת‏

22 ‏עוֹר וַיַּלְבִּשֵׁם: פ וַיֹּאמֶר ׀ יְהֹוָה אֱלֹהִים הֵן‏

‏הָאָדָם הָיָה כְּאַחַד מִמֶּנּוּ לָדַעַת טוֹב וָרָע וְעַתָּה ׀ פֶּן־‏

‏יִשְׁלַח יָדוֹ וְלָקַח גַּם מֵעֵץ הַחַיִּים וְאָכַל וָחַי לְעֹלָם:‏

23 ‏וַיְשַׁלְּחֵהוּ יְהֹוָה אֱלֹהִים מִגַּן־עֵדֶן לַעֲבֹד אֶת־הָאֲדָמָה‏

24 ‏אֲשֶׁר לֻקַּח מִשָּׁם: וַיְגָרֶשׁ אֶת־הָאָדָם וַיַּשְׁכֵּן מִקֶּדֶם‏

‏לְגַן־עֵדֶן אֶת־הַכְּרֻבִים וְאֵת לַהַט הַחֶרֶב הַמִּתְהַפֶּכֶת‏

‏לִשְׁמֹר אֶת־דֶּרֶךְ עֵץ הַחַיִּים: ס‏

‏מ‏ CAP. XL. ‏מ‏

א ‏וַיְהִי אַחַר הַדְּבָרִים הָאֵלֶּה חָטְאוּ מַשְׁקֵה מֶלֶךְ־מִצְרַיִם‏

2 ‏וְהָאֹפֶה לַאֲדֹנֵיהֶם לְמֶלֶךְ מִצְרָיִם: וַיִּקְצֹף פַּרְעֹה עַל שְׁנֵי‏

3 ‏סָרִיסָיו עַל שַׂר הַמַּשְׁקִים וְעַל שַׂר הָאוֹפִים: וַיִּתֵּן אֹתָם‏

‏בְּמִשְׁמַר בֵּית שַׂר הַטַּבָּחִים אֶל־בֵּית הַסֹּהַר מְקוֹם אֲשֶׁר‏

4 ‏יוֹסֵף אָסוּר שָׁם: וַיִּפְקֹד שַׂר הַטַּבָּחִים אֶת־יוֹסֵף אִתָּם‏

ה ‏וְשֵׁרֵת אֹתָם וַיִּהְיוּ יָמִים בְּמִשְׁמָר: וַיַּחַלְמוּ חֲלוֹם שְׁנֵיהֶם‎
‏אִישׁ חֲלֹמוֹ בְּלַיְלָה אֶחָד אִישׁ כְּפִתְרוֹן חֲלֹמוֹ הַמַּשְׁקֶה‎
‏וְהָאֹפֶה אֲשֶׁר לְמֶלֶךְ מִצְרַיִם אֲשֶׁר אֲסוּרִים בְּבֵית הַסֹּהַר:‎

ו ‏וַיָּבֹא אֲלֵיהֶם יוֹסֵף בַּבֹּקֶר וַיַּרְא אֹתָם וְהִנָּם זֹעֲפִים:‎

ז ‏וַיִּשְׁאַל אֶת־סְרִיסֵי פַרְעֹה אֲשֶׁר אִתּוֹ בְמִשְׁמַר בֵּית אֲדֹנָיו‎

ח ‏לֵאמֹר מַדּוּעַ פְּנֵיכֶם רָעִים הַיּוֹם: וַיֹּאמְרוּ אֵלָיו חֲלוֹם‎
‏חָלַמְנוּ וּפֹתֵר אֵין אֹתוֹ וַיֹּאמֶר אֲלֵהֶם יוֹסֵף הֲלוֹא לֵאלֹהִים‎

ט ‏פִּתְרֹנִים סַפְּרוּ־נָא לִי: וַיְסַפֵּר שַׂר־הַמַּשְׁקִים אֶת־חֲלֹמוֹ‎

י ‏לְיוֹסֵף וַיֹּאמֶר לוֹ בַּחֲלוֹמִי וְהִנֵּה־גֶפֶן לְפָנָי: וּבַגֶּפֶן שְׁלֹשָׁה‎
‏שָׂרִיגִם וְהִוא כְפֹרַחַת עָלְתָה נִצָּהּ הִבְשִׁילוּ אַשְׁכְּלֹתֶיהָ‎

יא ‏עֲנָבִים: וְכוֹס פַּרְעֹה בְּיָדִי וָאֶקַּח אֶת־הָעֲנָבִים וָאֶשְׂחַט‎
‏אֹתָם אֶל־כּוֹס פַּרְעֹה וָאֶתֵּן אֶת־הַכּוֹס עַל־כַּף פַּרְעֹה:‎

יב ‏וַיֹּאמֶר לוֹ יוֹסֵף זֶה פִּתְרֹנוֹ שְׁלֹשֶׁת הַשָּׂרִגִים שְׁלֹשֶׁת יָמִים‎

יג ‏הֵם: בְּעוֹד ׀ שְׁלֹשֶׁת יָמִים יִשָּׂא פַרְעֹה אֶת־רֹאשֶׁךָ וַהֲשִׁיבְךָ‎
‏עַל־כַּנֶּךָ וְנָתַתָּ כוֹס־פַּרְעֹה בְּיָדוֹ כַּמִּשְׁפָּט הָרִאשׁוֹן אֲשֶׁר‎

יד ‏הָיִיתָ מַשְׁקֵהוּ: כִּי אִם־זְכַרְתַּנִי אִתְּךָ כַּאֲשֶׁר יִיטַב לָךְ‎
‏וְעָשִׂיתָ־נָּא עִמָּדִי חָסֶד וְהִזְכַּרְתַּנִי אֶל־פַּרְעֹה וְהוֹצֵאתַנִי‎

טו ‏מִן־הַבַּיִת הַזֶּה: כִּי־גֻנֹּב גֻּנַּבְתִּי מֵאֶרֶץ הָעִבְרִים וְגַם־פֹּה‎

לֹא־עָשִׂיתִי מְא֔וּמָה כִּי־שָׂמ֥וּ אֹתִ֖י בַּבּֽוֹר: וַיַּ֥רְא שַׂר־הָאֹפִ֖ים 16

כִּי ט֣וֹב פָּתָ֑ר וַיֹּ֙אמֶר֙ אֶל־יוֹסֵ֔ף אַף־אֲנִי֙ בַּחֲלוֹמִ֔י וְהִנֵּ֕ה

שְׁלֹשָׁ֛ה סַלֵּ֥י חֹרִ֖י עַל־רֹאשִֽׁי: וּבַסַּ֣ל הָֽעֶלְי֗וֹן מִכֹּ֛ל מַאֲכַ֥ל 17

פַּרְעֹ֖ה מַעֲשֵׂ֣ה אֹפֶ֑ה וְהָע֗וֹף אֹכֵ֥ל אֹתָ֛ם מִן־הַסַּ֖ל מֵעַ֥ל

רֹאשִֽׁי: וַיַּ֤עַן יוֹסֵף֙ וַיֹּ֔אמֶר זֶ֖ה פִּתְרֹנ֑וֹ שְׁלֹ֙שֶׁת֙ הַסַּלִּ֔ים 18

שְׁלֹ֥שֶׁת יָמִ֖ים הֵֽם: בְּע֣וֹד ׀ שְׁלֹ֣שֶׁת יָמִ֗ים יִשָּׂ֤א פַרְעֹה֙ אֶת־ 19

רֹֽאשְׁךָ֙ מֵֽעָלֶ֔יךָ וְתָלָ֥ה אוֹתְךָ֖ עַל־עֵ֑ץ וְאָכַ֥ל הָע֛וֹף אֶת־

בְּשָׂרְךָ֖ מֵעָלֶֽיךָ: וַיְהִ֣י ׀ בַּיּ֣וֹם הַשְּׁלִישִׁ֗י י֚וֹם הֻלֶּ֣דֶת אֶת־ 20

פַּרְעֹ֔ה וַיַּ֥עַשׂ מִשְׁתֶּ֖ה לְכָל־עֲבָדָ֑יו וַיִּשָּׂ֞א אֶת־רֹ֣אשׁ ׀ שַׂ֣ר

הַמַּשְׁקִ֗ים וְאֶת־רֹ֛אשׁ שַׂ֥ר הָאֹפִ֖ים בְּת֥וֹךְ עֲבָדָֽיו: וַיָּ֕שֶׁב 21

אֶת־שַׂ֥ר הַמַּשְׁקִ֖ים עַל־מַשְׁקֵ֑הוּ וַיִּתֵּ֥ן הַכּ֖וֹס עַל־כַּ֥ף פַּרְעֹֽה:

וְאֵ֛ת שַׂ֥ר הָאֹפִ֖ים תָּלָ֑ה כַּאֲשֶׁ֥ר פָּתַ֛ר לָהֶ֖ם יוֹסֵֽף: וְלֹֽא־זָכַ֧ר 22 23

שַׂר־הַמַּשְׁקִ֛ים אֶת־יוֹסֵ֖ף וַיִּשְׁכָּחֵֽהוּ:

APPENDIX.

In compliance with the wishes of some of my students, I have here added a few pages containing some rules for the formation of the regular verb, together with the characteristics of the various parts of the verb, of the noun, and of the suffixes.

I. FORMATION OF THE REGULAR VERB.

1. The STEM of the verb is the third masc. sing. pret. Kal, and consists of three radical letters. The second radical is pointed with ־ָ, the vowel of action, the first radical receiving pretonic Kamets. (Green, § 82, 1.) קָטַל.

Intransitive verbs take ־ֵ or ־ָ with the second radical.

From the stem are next formed the six *conjugational stems*: viz.

(1) NIPHAL by prefixing Nun (נ) to the stem קָטַל. נִקְטַל which (Green, § 61, 1) becomes נִקְטַל.

(2) PIEL, by doubling the middle radical by Dagesh Forte (thus doubling or increasing the force of the verb), and pointing the first radical with ־ִ,* and the second with ־ֵ. קִטֵּל.

(3) PUAL, by doubling the middle radical, and pointing the first radical with ־ֻ, and the second with ־ַ. קֻטַּל.

(4) HIPHIL, by prefixing ה to the stem (in order to pronounce the vowel more strongly), and pointing it with ־ִ,* also placing ־ִי with the second radical. הִקְטִיל.

(5) HOPHAL, by prefixing ה pointed with ־ָ (or ־ֻ) to the stem. הָקְטַל.

(6) HITHPAEL, by prefixing הִת (the reflexive pronoun) to the original form of the Piel; viz. קַטֵּל. הִתְקַטֵּל.

---

* Contrary to the analogy of all the other forms of these Conjugations in Hebrew, as well as to *all* the forms of these Conjugations in each of the kindred languages.

2. From each of these seven stems is formed an *Infinitive absolute,* —

(a) In the *Kal* by changing the last vowel to וֹ. קָטוֹל.

(b) In the *Niphal* (sometimes by changing the last vowel of its stem to -, e.g. נִקְטֹל) generally by prefixing ה (a relic of הָן) to the stem, assimilating the נ and representing it by Dagesh Forte (הִקָּטֹל), inserting pretonic ָ under the first radical (הִקָּטֹל), and changing the ult. vowel of the stem to Cholem; e.g. הִקָּטֹל.

(c) In the *Piel* and *Pual*, by changing the ult. vowel of the stems to -, and in the Piel by placing the original vowel of its stem, (viz. Pattach), under the first radical; e.g. קָטֹל, קֻטֹּל.

(d) In the *Hiphil* and *Hophal*, by changing the ult. vowel of the stems to Tsūrā (-), and in the Hiphil by restoring the original vowel, i.e. -, to the prefix ה; e.g, הָקְטֵל, הַקְטֵיל.

(e) In the *Hithpael*, by changing the ult. vowel of the stem to Cholem; e.g. הִתְקַטֹּל.

REMARK. — It will be noted, therefore, that *Cholem in the ult.* usually marks the *Infinitive absolute.*

3. From each Infinitive absolute is next formed an *Infinitive construct,* —

(a) In the *Kal* by rejecting the pretonic Kamets.

(b) In the *Niphal* by changing - to -.

(c) In all the other Conjugations by changing the ult. vowel so as to correspond with the ult. vowel of its conjugational stem.

4. From each *Infinitive construct* is formed a *Future;* by prefixing the personal preformatives י, ת, א, נ, dropping the ה of the Inf. in Niph., Hiph., Hoph., and Hithpael, and giving its vowel to the personal prefix.

These prefixes, abstractly considered, are of course pointed with Sh°va.

5. From the second person of the *Jussive Future* (Green, § 97, 2) in *all* cases are formed the *Imperatives*, by simply dropping the personal prefix תִ (which is superfluous in the Imp.) and restoring the ה if it originally stood in the Infinitive construct.

The Pual and Hophal being pure passives, have no Imperative.

6. The *participles* (being verbal *nouns*) are mostly formed from the *Infinitive construct.*

(a) In the *Kal*, however, the arbitrary forms קָטֵל קָטוּל are used.

(b) In the Niphal the form נִקְטָל (formed after the analogy of the participles of intransitive verbs, i.e. from the conjugational stem) is used.

(c) In the other Conjugations מ is prefixed to the Infinitive, the ה is dropped, the מ taking its vowel instead of ־ְ, and the last vowel of the Infinitive, if short, is lengthened.

TABULAR VIEW OF THE REGULAR VERB, to illustrate these rules.

	Kal.	Niphal.	Piel.	Pual.	Hiphil.	Hophal.	Hithpael.
Stems	קָטַל	נִקְטַל	קִטֵּל	קֻטַּל	הִקְטִיל	הָקְטַל	הִתְקַטֵּל
Inf. abs.	קָטוֹל	הִקָּטֹל	קַטֵּל	קֻטֹּל	הַקְטֵל	הָקְטֵל	הִתְקַטֵּל
Inf. con.	קְטֹל	הִקָּטֵל	קַטֵּל	קֻטַּל	הַקְטִיל	הָקְטַל	הִתְקַטֵּל
Futures	יִקְטֹל	יִקָּטֵל	יְקַטֵּל	יְקֻטַּל	יַקְטִיל	יָקְטַל	יִתְקַטֵּל
Impera.	קְטֹל	הִקָּטֵל	קַטֵּל		הַקְטֵל		הִתְקַטֵּל
Particip.	קֹטֵל	נִקְטָל	מְקַטֵּל	מְקֻטָּל	מַקְטִיל	מָקְטָל	מִתְקַטֵּל
	קָטוּל						

For the explanation of the personal *affixes* of the Perfect or Preterite, and of the *prefixes* of the Future, cf. Green, § 85, 1. a., and for the vowel changes, cf. § 85, 2. a.

II CHARACTERISTICS OF THE VERB.

In looking at a form of the verb, having removed its suffixes, first determine its *tense* or *mode*.

1. CHARACTERISTICS OF THE TENSES.

The *Future* may be known by its *prefix* נ, ת, י, א.

The *Perfect* has *affixes*, but no personal prefixes.

REM. — The *Imperative* also takes affixes, but cannot be mistaken for the Perfect, as the vowels under the first radical in the Kal and Piel, and under the ה in Hiph., and Hith., differ; while in the Niph. the Imper. takes the prefix ה, the Perf. having נ.

2. CONJUGATIONAL CHARACTERISTICS.

(A) If a verb be in the *Future*, the *vowel under the prefix* marks the Conjugation.

This vowel in the *regular* verb, in the *Kal* and *Niphal* is ־ִ, in *Piel* and *Pual* invariably ־ְ, in *Hiphil* ־ַ, in *Hophal* ־ָ or ־ֻ, in *Hithpael*, הִ־.

The *Niphal* may be distinguished from *Kal*, by the ־ָ under the first Radical immediately after the prefix. יִקְטֹל יִקָּטֵל. The *Piel* from the *Pual* by the vowels under the first radical.

8

As these vowels under the prefixes are, in the various classes of verbs, liable to mutations caused by the presence of weak letters, etc., the following table may be found useful in most cases, not only for determining in what *conjugation* the *future* tense of a verb is found, but also to what *class* it belongs, thus serving the student as guide for tracing out the root.

Class.	Kal.	Niphal.	Piel.	Pual.	Hiphil.	Hophal.	Hithpael.
Reg. Verb,	־ (ֱ)*	־ (ֱ)*	־ (ֱ)*	־ (ֱ)*	־	ָ (ֳ)	הִ־
‍ע guttural,							
ל guttural,							
לא							
פֹ							ֳ
פ guttural,	־ ֳ	־					
פא	־ ֳ	־					
לה	(ֳ apoc. form.)						
פי	־ יָ			׀ (יָ)	ו		
עע	ָ (־ ־)				ָ	ו (ָ)	
פו	ָ				ֵ	ו	

* These occur only under א. The other vowels in brackets occur only in exceptional forms. Where no vowels are printed the vowels are the same as in the Regular Verb.

It will be be observed that the vowel under the prefixes of the Future varies chiefly in the Kal, Hiphil, and Hophal Conjugations.

To illustrate the method of using this table, take יוֹשִׁיב: the vowel with the prefix is יִ; referring to the table we find that the conjugation is *Hiphil*, and, casting the eye to the left hand column, that it is a פי verb; יָשַׁב is therefore the root.

Or, take יָקוּם. The vowel of the prefix is ־ָ, therefore, by the table, the form is in the *Kal* or *Hiphil* conjugations, and the verb belongs to the class עע or עו. The vowel ־ִי or ־ִ under the *radical*, will readily distinguish the *Hiphil* from the *Kal* in these classes of verbs; e.g. Kal רָקוּם, Hiphil יָקִים; Kal יָסֹב, Hiphil יָסֵב.

(B) If the verb (having an *affix*) be in the *Preterite*,
נ prefixed marks the *Niphal*,
Dagesh Forte in the middle Radical marks the *Piel* and *Pual*.

　Exc. Verbs ע guttural, of course omit the Dagesh, but lengthen the vowel under the first Radical to ־ֵ in the Piel, and to ־ֹ in the Pual; e.g. Piel בֵּרֵ֫ךְ, Pual גֹּרַל. Verbs עו double the *third* Radical, which form verbs עע borrow.

ה prefixed marks the *Hiphil* and *Hophal*.
הִתְ prefixed marks the *Hithpael*.

3. CHARACTERISTICS OF THE PERSON.

PRETERITE Tense. 　*Affix* ־ִי or נוּ denotes the 1st person.
　　　　　　　　Affix תָ, תְ, תֶּם, תֶּן denotes the 2d person.
　　　　　　　　Affix ־ָה or וּ denotes the 3d person.
FUTURE Tense. 　*Prefix* א or נ denotes the 1st person.
　　　　　　　　Prefix ת denotes the 2d person.
　　　　　　　　Prefix י (or ת) denotes the 3d person.

4. CHARACTERISTICS OF NUMBER.

Affixes נָה, ן, וּ, ם denote the *Plural*.

5. CHARACTERISTICS OF THE INFINITIVE AND IMPERATIVE.

Infinitives and Imperatives have the *conjugation* denoted as in the *Preterite*, except the *Niphal*, which takes the prefix ה and also Dagesh Forte in the first Radical, except in verbs פ guttural.

6. CHARACTERISTICS OF THE PARTICIPLES.

Niphal Participle begins with נ; all the rest (except Kal) with מ, and the conjugation is denoted as in the *Future*, i.e. by the vowel accompanying the prefix.

III. CHARACTERISTICS OF THE NOUN.
MASCULINE.
Singular.

Absolute has no characteristic termination.

Construct is like the Absolute; except in case there is a mutable vowel in the Absolute it is generally shortened or rejected.

NOTE. — Kamets and Tsara rarely occur in the construct.

Nouns in הָ‑ make their Construct in הֵ‑.

Nouns in יִ‑ make their Construct in יֵ‑.

Plural.

Absolute ends in ‑ים (rarely in ‑ִין or ‑ֵי).

NOTE. — Some masculines make their plural in וֹת (cf. Green § 200 a.).

Segholates insert ‑ָ before ‑ים; e.g. מְלָכִים.

Construct ends in ‑ֵי.

FEMININE.
Singular.

Absolute ends in הָ‑ or הַ‑ (rarely in ‑ָא, ‑ֶה, ‑ֶת).

Construct ends in ‑ַת (or ‑ָת).

Plural.

Absolute. וֹת is substituted for the ending of the Singular.

Segholates insert ‑ָ before this ending וֹת.

Construct also ends in וֹת, before which Segholates revert to their original monosyllabic form.

Duals make their *Absolute* in ‑ַיִם, their *Construct* in ‑ֵי. Before ‑ַיִם feminines in הָ‑ become ‑ָת.

IV. CHARACTERISTICS OF THE PRONOMINAL SUFFIXES.

First Person is indicated by י or נ.

Second Person is indicated by ך.

Third Person is indicated by הָ‑, ו, ם, or ן.

NOTE. — י inserted between a noun and its suffix shows that the *noun* is in the *plural* number; in the first person singular this י coincides with the characteristic of the suffix.

If the characteristics as here given are thoroughly committed to memory, it is believed that, in most cases, the student will, with his previous study of the Grammar, be able to analyze a word at sight.

TERMINATIONS OF NOMINAL FORMS.

		SINGULAR.		PLURAL.		DUAL.	
		Absolute.	Construct.	Absolute.	Construct.	Absolute.	Construct.
MASCULINE.		No characteristic ending.	Like Absolute.	} ים֖	י֑֖	־ַ֫יִם	־֫יֵ
		ה֖	ה֑֖				
		י֑	י֑				
		י֑	י֑	־ַ֖יִים (or ־֑ים)	־ַ֫יֵ		
		Segholates.	Like Absolute.	־ַ֑ים	י֑		
FEMININE.		ה֖	} ת֑	} ות	ות	־ַ֫תַיִם	־ַ֫תֵי
		*ת֑	ת֑				
		†ת֑					
		ת֑	ת֑	־֫יוֹת	־֫יוֹת		
		ות	ות	־֑יוֹת	־֑יוֹת		
		*ת֑	} No Construct.	No Plural.			
		*א֑					
		Segholates.	ת֑ or ת֑	־ֹות֑	ות		

* These terminations are very rare.

† Nouns in ה֑ are not treated as Segholates.

This Table gives the *usual* endings of the Noun according to its different *Numbers, Genders,* and *States.* Through these endings the noun may be traced back to its Absolute Singular.

N.B. — The *Masculine* Plural termination is *added to* the Absolute Singular. The *Feminine* Plural ending וֹת is *substituted for* the Feminine Singular termination.

Before making use of the Table all suffixes and prefixes must be removed from the noun. Note, that all nouns which occur with a suffix are in the *Construct* State.

The *Construct* Sing. Masc. and the *Construct* Plural Fem. may often be distinguished from the Absolute by the brevity of the vowels. Kamets seldom, and Tsara infrequently occur in the Construct.

Form for parsing a *Verb*. — First analyze the form, taking off Suffixes, Vav Conv., Prep., etc. Then give Root; Synopsis of the seven Conjugations; Tense; Person; Number; Gender; Conjugation; Syntax.

Form for parsing a *Noun*. — Analyze; give the Abs. Sing.; Abs. and Const. Sing. and Plural; Case; Number; State; Syntax.

For *Suffixes*. — Number; Person; Gender; Case.

For *Participles*. — Give Stem; Synopsis of Conj.; Conj.; Abs. and Const., Sing. and Plural; Number; State; Syntax.

For the convenience of the student the characteristics of the various forms of the Verb and Noun, as given in detail above, are summed up in the Tabular Views on p. 61 and pp. 66, 67. The method of using the Tabular View of the Verb is indicated on pp. 58, 59 (cf. Table there given).

With the Table open before him, the student can not only determine the *tense, conjugation*, etc., of almost any verb he meets with in the Hebrew Bible, but is also guided to the *root* for which he is to consult his lexicon. The Table serves for all classes of verbs; irregularities, anomalies, etc., being, of course excepted.

The Table of Nominal Forms (p. 61) while giving the endings for gender, number, and state, may also serve to indicate the form which is to sought for in the lexicon.

TO FIND WORDS IN THE LEXICON.

In addition to the Tables of Verbal and Nominal Characteristics, the following rules will supply the student with the necessary information for finding words in the Lexicon.

I. Nouns. Reject from the word all prefixes (e.g. בּ, כּ, לְ, מ, ה, שׁ, וּ), all suffixes, and plural or dual terminations.

II. Verbs. 1. All verbal roots are *tri-literal*. To obtain this root,

(A) Reject from the *beginning* of the form, (1) all personal prefixes, י, ת, נ, א; (2) all conjugational preformatives, נ, ה, הִתְ; (3) the participial prefix, מ; (4) the prefix prepositions, בּ, כּ, פ, לְ, מ; (5) the article [sometimes prefixed to the participle] and interrogative particle, ה; (6) the relative, שׁ; and (7) ו copulative or conversive.

(B) Reject from the *end* of the form all personal affixes (נִי, חֶן, הֶם, ו, ר, י, ת, ךָ), suffixes, and paragogic letters.

(C) Reject all *inserted* letters, as וֹ, ־ִי, ־ֵ, ־ֶ.

2. If after the form is thus divested of its servile letters, *three* letters be left, they are the root.

3. If but *two* letters are left, then the verb is defective, and wants, (1) an *initial* י or נ; (2) a *medial* ו or י; (3) *final* ה (very seldom א); or the second radical must be doubled.

A knowledge of the Paradigms of the verbs will enable the student to determine generally the Class to which the verb before him must belong. Dagesh Forte, however, in the first of the remaining radicals generally denotes the absence of initial נ (rarely י).

Vav (ו, וֹ, or וּ) after the personal or conjugational prefix usually represents initial י.

The inserted vowel (וֹ, וּ, or ־ִי) often serve to indicate עע or עי verbs.

If after rejection, as in (A), (B), (C), י remains as the third radical, the verb is לה.

Dagesh Forte in the *second* of the remaining radicals will frequently point out an עע verb.

4. If but *one* letter is left, prefix נ (rarely י) and add ה.

N.B.— When ו Conversive of the Future is removed, the prefix that follows it must also be removed with it.

The following mnemonic lines by Tregelles may be found of use:

> "The servile letters cast away,
> And if behind *three* letters stay
> You'll have the root without delay.
> But if you have not letters three,
> The root will then defective be.
> Perhaps the root you seek is one
> Which *drops initial Yothe or Noon:*
> A *medial Yothe or Vav* may show
> The letters three you want to know:
> Perhaps the letter which stands second,
> To make the three, *must twice be reckoned:*
> Or, finally, perhaps you may
> Require to add a final Hay."

TABULAR VIEW OF THE CHARACTERISTICS OF THE VERB.

PERFECT TENSE.

CLASS.	KAL.	NIPHAL.	PIEL.	PUAL.	HIPHIL.	HOPHAL.	HITHPAEL.
Regular,		נ prefixed.	Dag. Forte in 2d Radical.	Dag. Forte in 2d Radical.	הִ prefixed.	הָ prefixed.	הִת prefixed.
ע guttural,			Dagesh Forte omitted; 1st Radical has ֵ	Dagesh Forte omitted; 1st Radical has —			
פנ		נ pref. Dag.F. Comp. in 2d Rad.					
עו			1st Radical has וֹ; 3d Radical doubled.	1st Radical has וֹ; 3d Radical doubled.			
עע			1st Radical has וֹ	1st Radical has וֹ			

IMPERATIVE (2 m. s.) AND INFINITIVE CONSTRUCT.

CLASS.	KAL.	NIPHAL.	PIEL.	PUAL.	HIPHIL.	HOPHAL.	HITHPAEL.
Regular,	ֹ in ult. syllable. (rarely ֵ)	Prefix הִ	Dag. Forte in 2d Radical.	Dagesh Forte omitted; 1st Radical has ֵ	הַ prefixed.	הָ prefixed.	הִת prefixed.
פ gut. and אפ		Prefix הֵ					
ע guttural,				Dagesh Forte omitted; 1st Radical has ֵ			
פנ and פי	lose 1st Rad.		1st Radical has וֹ	1st Radical has וֹ			
עו		No ֵ under 1st Radical.	1st Radical has וֹ	1st Radical has וֹ			
עע	generally takes וֹ	No ֵ under 1st Radical.	1st Radical has וֹ; 3d Radical doubled.	1st Radical has וֹ; 3d Radical doubled.			

FUTURE TENSE.

N.B. The Vowel under the Prefix is the mark of the Future.

Regular,	◌ֵ	* (◌ַ) ◌ֹ	◌ִ	◌ֵ	◌ַ (ō) or ◌ֵ	◌ַ
פ״ן	[Apoc. form sometimes has ◌ֵ]				
ע״ע					
פ guttural,	◌ַ or ◌ֶ	◌ַ◌ or ◌ֶ			◌ֶ
פ״א	◌ֹ (or ◌ֵ)	◌ֹ (or ◌ֵ)			
פ״י	◌ֵ (or ◌ֶ)	◌ֵ (or ◌ֶ)		◌ֵ (or ◌ֶ)	◌ֵ
ע״ו	◌ָ (or ◌ֹ or ◌ַ)	No ◌ַ under 1st Radical.		◌ָ	◌ָ
ל״ה or ל״י	◌ַ	No ◌ַ under first Radical.		◌ָ	◌ָ	◌ַ

PARTICIPLES.

	◌ֵ◌	◌ֻ◌ ◌ָ◌	נ prefixed.	מ with same vowel as Future.	מ with same vowel as Future.	מֻ◌ prefixed

* Note that the Future Niphal always has ◌ַ under the First Radical after the Vowel of the Prefix, except Verbs ע״ע and פ״ו.

The Future is always known by the *Prefix* (א י ת נ). The Perfect is always known by the *Affix* (ת—, תָ, תְ, תִי, נוּ, תֶם, ן).

The Imperative and Future also have the *Affixes* י—, ו, נָה. The Perfect and Imperative have no personal prefixes.

The *First* Person is marked by א or נ prefixed, or by תִי or נוּ affixed.   The *Second* Person is marked by ת prefixed or affixed.

The *Third* Person is marked by י (or ת) prefixed, or ת— or ה affixed.   PLURALS are known by the endings תָ, יִ, ו, חֶם.

N.B.—The Characteristics of all classes of Verbs in their several parts are almost always like those of the *Regular* Verb, with the exceptions noted in the above Tabular View.

A

HARMONY OF THE FOUR GOSPELS

IN GREEK,

ACCORDING TO THE TEXT OF TISCHERDORF; WITH A COLLATION OF THE
TEXTUS RECEPTUS, AND OF THE TEXTS OF GRIESBACH, LACHMANN,
AND TREGELLES.

BY

FREDERIC GARDINER, D.D.,

PROFESSOR IN THE BERKELEY DIVINITY SCHOOL, AUTHOR OF "A COMMENTARY ON THE
EPISTLE OF ST. JUDE," "A HARMONY OF THE GOSPELS IN ENGLISH," ETC.

8vo.   pp. lvi and 268.   Price, $2.50.

The distinctive features of this Harmony are, —

1. A critical text. viz. the text of Tischendorf's eighth or last edition, embodying
the latest results of textual criticism.   To obtain the final portions of this edition
the publication of this work has been delayed several months.   The readings of
the *textus receptus*, where they differ from Tischendorf's text, are given in full in
the margin; the variations being designated by a different type.   The texts of
Griesbach, Lachman, and Tregelles are carefully collated.   The relative value of
readings as estimated by Griesbach are noted, and original authorities cited in
important cases.

2. All distinct quotations from the Old Testament are given in full in the
margin, according to Tischendorf's edition of the LXX., together with the *var.
lect.* of the Alexandrian text and of the *Codex Sinaiticus*, and of the several other
versions named in the title.

3. A choice selection of parallel references has been placed in the margin, chiefly
to point out similar language or incidents in other parts of the Gospels, or passages
in the Old Testament, on which the language of the Gospels may be founded.

4. Brief notes relating to matters of harmony have been placed at the bottom
of the page.

5. Special care has been devoted to the chronological order of the Gospel
narratives.

6. The columns are so arranged on the page as to combine the greatest clearness
consistent with the least cost.   The columns are never interwoven on the page.

7. A synoptical table is given of the arrangement adopted by several harmonists,
showing at a glance the general agreement on the main points of chronology, and
the points of difference where difference occurs.   This is a new feature in this
work, and will be found very useful to the student.

WARREN F. DRAPER, Publisher,
Andover, Mass.

31

A

HARMONY OF THE FOUR GOSPELS
IN ENGLISH,

ACCORDING TO THE AUTHORIZED VERSION; CORRECTED BY THE BEST
CRITICAL EDITIONS OF THE ORIGINAL.

By FREDERIC GARDINER, D.D.,

PROFESSOR IN THE BERKELEY DIVINITY SCHOOL; AUTHOR OF "A HARMONY OF THE
GOSPELS IN GREEK," ETC.

8vo.   pp. xliv and 287.   Price, $2.00.

This Harmony is a reproduction in English of the author's "Harmony of the
Four Gospels" in Greek. Being intended for English readers, so much of the
Introduction and of the notes as require a knowledge of Greek, is omitted. Other
notes have been abridged in many cases.

DIATESSARON.

THE

LIFE OF OUR LORD;
IN
The Words of the Gospels.

By FREDERIC GARDINER, D.D.,

PROFESSOR IN THE BERKELEY DIVINITY SCHOOL, AUTHOR OF "A HARMONY OF THE GOSPELS IN
GREEK," ETC. ETC.

16mo.   pp. 259.   Price, $1.00.

This work combines in one continuous narrative the events of the life of Christ
as recorded by all the evangelists. His genealogy, conversations, discourses,
parables, miracles, his trial, death, resurrection, and ascension, are placed in the
order of their occurrence ; and in the foot-notes references are made to passages in
the Old Testament relating to Christ or quoted by him.

The life of our Lord has been of late years presented in such a multitude of
forms, colored with the views and theories of such a multitude of minds, that it is
hoped the present effort to present that life in the exact form of the inspired record,
without addition or abatement, may tend to the increase of the real knowledge of
the life of the Saviour of mankind.

The work is specially adapted for use in the family and in Sabbath-schools and
Bible-classes.

W. F. DRAPER, Publisher,

Andover, Mass.

MEDIATION.

THE FUNCTION OF THOUGHT.

16mo.   Small Pica Type.   pp. 213.   Price, $1.25.

This volume forms one part or chapter of a larger proposed work under the title of "Thoughts on Mediation; or, the Relation of Christ to the World." The author reasons that as Christ and his apostles claim the reasonableness of his doctrine, and appeal to the honest conviction of men for its acceptance, we may justly inquire for the solution of this problem; or, that the truths evolved by the doctrine of Mediation will throw strong lights on everything touched by them, and give new significance to all we conceived before.

The author proposes in this volume to show the base which exists in the normal constitution of humanity for the doctrine of Mediation; and also that this base is as wide and as universal as the whole scope of human thought. He proceeds with a profound and suggestive discussion of the function of thought in man as distinguishing him from all other animals, not only in degree but in kind. These specific functions are classed as, I. That of Language. II. Proportion, or the relation of forms, subdivided under three heads, — Pure Mathematics, Applied Science, and Art. III. Jurisprudence or Law. In all which man is not only superior, but essentially different from all the animals. By language he has general ideas, society; through proportion he has form, beauty, art, mathematics; from law, order, government, morals.

A MEMORIAL

OF

SAMUEL HARVEY TAYLOR.

COMPILED BY HIS LAST CLASS.

8vo. pp. 127. Pica Type. Tinted paper; cloth, bevelled, gilt edges. Published by Subscription. Price, $1.75.

This elegant litle volume is a tribute of affection and respect to the late Principal of Phillips Academy, by his last Senior Class. It contains the Address by Professor Park, at the Funeral of Dr. Taylor; the Selection from the Scriptures read on the occasion by Prof. J. L. Taylor; a Sermon by Prof. J. W. Churchill, preached at the Chapel of the Theological Seminary on the Sabbath following; Resolutions of the Members of the Academy and the Alumni, with some account of the Funeral Services, and Reminiscences by a former pupil. A beautiful Photograph, cabinet size, the last one taken of Dr. Taylor, precedes the title.

A few copies only are for sale.

AN ADDRESS,

DELIVERED AT THE

FUNERAL OF SAMUEL HARVEY TAYLOR, LL.D.

BY EDWARDS A. PARK.

From the Bibliotheca Sacra for April. 8vo. pp. 33. Paper covers. Price, 25 cents.

W. F. DRAPER, Publisher,

Andover, Mass.

CLASSICAL STUDY: Its Usefulness illustrated by Selections from the Writings of Eminent Scholars. Edited, with an Introduction, by SAMUEL H. TAYLOR, LL.D., Principal of Phillips Academy. 12mo. pp. 415. Cloth extra, Price, $2.00.

Professor *J. R. Boise, of the University of Chicago*, thus writes in the March number of the *Illinois Teacher*: "The selection of essays made by Dr. Taylor is eminently judicious, and presents the views of many leading writers, both in Europe and in this country. The Introduction, containing about thirty pages, gives, first, a concise and clear sketch of the history of the controversy on the value of classical studies; and then, several reasons why the highest benefits of classical study are seldom reached in this country. On this latter point, we know of no one better qualified by education and long experience as a teacher to speak wisely. This collection of essays reminds us of one feature in the whole controversy with which we have often been struck: the readiness of classical men to concede an honorable position to scientific studies. There have been few exceptions to this rule; whereas, scientific men have not unfrequently demanded for their favorite pursuits the entire field, to the exclusion of everything else; at least, to the entire exclusion of the ancient languages. . . . . . To all who desire the best collection of essays in our language on classical study, the work of Dr. Taylor will be very welcome. It should have a conspicuous place in every school-library, and in the private library of every educator in our land."

In another connection Prof. Boise adds: "Not the least valuable part of the volume is the Introduction, in which Dr. Taylor so ably, clearly, and fairly balances the arguments on the two sides. The conception of the entire work was a happy thought, and is carried out with that good judgment which I long ago learned to expect from him."

Dr. McCosh, President of Princeton College writes: "I value exceedingly your admirable work. The selection seems to me to be judicious, and the general impression left by the perusal is excellent. The work is fitted to do much good. I wish it were known in Great Britain, where there is a strong anti-classical reaction."

Professor Goodwin, of Harvard University, in a note to the Author, thus expresses his appreciation of the work: "You have done an excellent and a most timely service; and I am sure it will do good in counteracting much of the ignorant and nonsensical talk which we hear about the classics. The most ignorant form in which the opposition to the classics appears is when it uses such essays as those of Farrar's as arguments against our system of classical study in America; as if it could be affected by such arguments, even allowing them to be good over against the English system."

Professor George B. Jewett, in a letter to Dr. Taylor, speaks of the work thus: "Most effectually have you, by your own pen and by the writings of others, met and refuted, in this volume the numerous objections to classical study which that groundless prejudice is constantly reiterating; most nobly have you illustrated the value of the pursuit. At first the plan of your work seemed to me to involve much of unavoidable repetition, without securing a corresponding depth of impression. But a careful reading of the book has convinced me of the peculiar excellence of your plan, and, in fact, that it leaves nothing to be regretted, unless, perhaps, that the space occupied by your own pen is so greatly disproportionate to that which you have awarded to others. So far is the book from becoming wearisome by its repetitions, that it is quite kaleidoscopic in the variety and fascination of the views which it presents. It must carry conviction to all who will read it candidly, and who are capable of appreciating its multiform proofs and illustrations. It cannot fail to give a fresh impulse to the cause it so ably advocates. It will serve as a repository of facts and arguments from which inexhaustible supplies may be drawn for the defense and vindication of this sorely abused department of study. For furnishing this storehouse you are entitled to the thanks of all who are striving to promote the interest of sound learning."

President Aiken of Union College says: "It more than meets my expectation, and I am sure will render a valuable and timely service to the cause of good learning. It will prove a rich storehouse of arguments and illustrations for those who believe in the old ways."

"We think Dr. Taylor has made a good fight, and that opponents will have much to do to sustain the onset, if they are not completely unhorsed." — *Philadelphia Paper*.

"We commend the book as a valuable collection of essays on the higher methods of mental training." — *American Presbyterian*.

"We are glad that our friend, Dr. Taylor, the learned and eminent Principal of what we conceive to be, on the whole, the best training school in New England, has thought it wise to bring together into a comely volume, a series of more than twenty testimonies and arguments, from some of the ablest thinkers of the age, in favor of the thorough critical and continuous study of the Greek and Roman classics — prefaced by an apt and convincing discussion of his own. Dr. Taylor thus has gathered together some of the ripest thoughts and most valuable suggestions of Mr. Principal Jones, Prof. Thiersch, Hugh S. Legaré, Dr. Whewell, John Stuart Mill, Prof. Noah Porter, Joseph Payne, Prof. B. B. Edwards, Prof. John Conington, Wm. Howard Gardiner, Esq., Prof. Pillans, Dr. Geo. B. Loring, Prof. Sellar, Pres. McCosh, Prof. E. D. Sanborn, Prof Masson, Hon. P. H. Sears, Pres. Felton, Pres. Brown, Prof. D'Arcy W. Thompson, Prof. Goldwin Smith, and Prof. L. Campbell. There is a charm in being able to note so readily the different moving of so many minds upon one such subject as this; as well as great significance and force in the verdict in which such a jury agree." — *Congregationalist*.

WARREN F. DRAPER, Publisher,

ANDOVER, MASS.

MISCELLANEOUS WORKS

WARREN F. DRAPER,

ANDOVER, MASS.

These Books will be sent, post-paid, on receipt of the price affixed.

CLASSICAL STUDY : Its Usefulness illustrated by Selections from the Writings of Eminent Scholars. Edited, with an Introduction, by SAMUEL H. TAYLOR, LL.D., Principal of Phillips Academy. 12mo. pp. 415. Cloth extra. $2.00

This work is designed to present the true objects of Classical Study, and the advantages of it when properly conducted; also to correct the objections which have been raised against the study. It consists of extracts from some of the best critics on classical education in Germany, England, Scotland, and our own country; the writers themselves being presidents of colleges, professors in colleges and theological seminaries, statesmen, lawyers, etc. In the volume therefore will be found the carefully-framed opinions of many of the best minds of the time. No one line of thought has been taken; the subject has been viewed from almost every point. The work therefore contains a fuller discussion of the advantages of classical study than has before been accessible. The need of such a volume is widely felt among the friends of sound learning. Every student as he commences his classical course should understand what he is to aim at and what he is to gain by the study.

ΦΩΚΥΛΙΔΟΥ ΠΟΙΗΜΑ ΝΟΥΘΕΤΙΚΟΝ. PHOCYLIDIS POEMA ADMONI-TORIUM. Recognovit Brevibusque Notis Instruxit. J. B. FEULING, Ph.D., A.O.S.S., Professor Philologiae Compar. in Univer. Wisconsinensi. Editio Prima Americana. 16mo. pp. 32. Paper, 30 cents ; gilt edges, 40 cents.

"Warren F. Draper, of Andover, publishes Prof. J. B. Feuling's *Phocylidis Poema Admonitorium*, with a double introduction and a few notes, all in Latin; the poem itself, however, is in the original Greek, and is a collection of moral sentences after the manner of Phocylides, in hexameter verse, which was probably compiled some eight centuries after the poet's death, though nobody knows when. Scaliger thought it quite as good as anything the old Milesian ever wrote, and very likely it is; but in language it differs from the genuine hexameter of the Ionian school of poets to which Theognis and Solon belonged. The main introduction of the author relates chiefly to classical studies in America, and the late convention "in urbe quam vocant Poughkeepsie," to which, by anticipation, he dedicates his little book. His notes are valuable for the citations from Theognis, Epictetus, Simplicius, Sophocles, Euripides, Epicharneus, Terence, Cicero, Sallust, Horace, and Ovid; some of which are rare, and all apposite."—*Springfield Republican*.

THE THEOLOGY OF THE GREEK POETS. By W. S. TYLER, Williston Professor of Greek in Amherst College. 12mo. pp. 365. Cloth, bevelled. $1.75

"Professor Tyler has here produced a work which is an honor to American literature. It is well fitted to be a classic in our Colleges and Theological Seminaries. It furnishes admirable illustrations of the truth of both natural and revealed theology, and suggests original methods for the defence of these truths." — *Bibliotheca Sacra*.
"The aim of the author is to detect the analogies between the myths of the Greek drama and epic, and the truths of revelation. The care of the scholar and the enthusiasm of the poet have been given to the work." — *Independent*.
"Prof. Tyler has done good service to the cause of truth in showing that the Iliad and Odyssey, as well as the dramas of Aeschylus and the tragedies of Sophocles, express ideas and sentiments very much like those we find in contemporary Scriptures."—*Hours at Home*.

LECTURES ON PASTORAL THEOLOGY. By ENOCH POND, D.D., Professor in Bangor Theological Seminary. Second Ed. 12mo. pp. 395. $1.75

"This volume is an excellent and practical treatise upon pastoral duty, and is heartily commended to all who are entering upon or engaged in the holy office of the Christian ministry." — *New York Observer*.
"Though especially adapted to Congregational churches and ministers, they will be found of use to all; for they are wise and prudent. All the special relations and duties of the ministry are fully and clearly discussed." — *American Presbyterian Theological Review*.

i

Goodrich. Bible History of Prayer. By C. A. GOODRICH. 12mo.
pp, 384. $1.25

"The aim of this little volume is to embody an account of the delightful and successful intercourse of believers with heaven for some four thousand years. The author has indulged a good deal in narrative, opening and explaining the circumstances which gave birth to the several prayers.

"The author does not aim to write a treatise on prayer, or to comment on all the references to prayer in chronological order, but to dwell on its nature and importance, and make suggestions on the most important allusions to prayer, as indicated all along for four thousand years. He explains the circumstances connected with the prayers of these holy men." — *Religious Union.*

Hebrew English Psalter. ספר תהלים. The Book of Psalms, in Hebrew and English, arranged in parallelism. 16mo. pp. 194. $1.50

"The neat little volume which bears the above title may be briefly characterized as a happy idea beautifully executed. The Hebrew Text of the Psalms is divided according to the poetical pause-points of the verses, so that it appears in lines as sung by the Jewish cantillators. The Hebrew text according to Hahn, with Rosenmüller's arrangement, in parallel clauses, occupies one column, and the English text of the Common Version another; the two standing side by side, so that, as far as the idioms of the two languages admit, the corresponding Hebrew and English clauses stand opposite to each other. In the few cases where the different order followed in the version makes such a parallelism impossible, it is indicated by braces enclosing the translation.

"The preacher in expounding to his congregation one of the Psalms of David, will find it very convenient to have the original by the side of the English version. For private reading and meditation, also, such an arrangement will be found very pleasant and profitable. We feel confident that this little volume will be a favorite with Hebrew scholars ; and that, when they have once become habituated to it, it will be, to many of them, a *vade mecum.*" — *Bibliotheca Sacra.*

"To the devout scholar who loves to see these sacred songs of the temple worship written as they were chanted, and desires to possess a correct arrangement of the alphabetical Psalms, this little book is invaluable." — *Watchman and Reflector.*

"The book is compact, well-printed, and every way adapted to its purpose." — *Lutheran and Missionary.*

"A happy design, and beautifully executed in its typography." — *Boston Review.*

"A handsome edition of the book of Psalms, which will be quite a favorite with clergymen and theological students." — *New Englander.*

"A very convenient and admirable manual, and we beg leave to thank our Andover friend for it." — *Presbyterian Quarterly.*

"This beautifully printed work will be very popular with biblical scholars. It is portable, and to one who has become measurably acquainted with the original, it must be a valuable *vade mecum.*" — *Methodist Quarterly.*

"We have here a beautifully clear and eye-comforting edition of the Hebrew Psalter, according to Hahn's text, but arranged in verse mostly according to Rosenmüller. ..... Every lover of the Hebrew will desire and be grateful for so agreeable a help to his studies and devotions." — *Congregationalist.*

"The volume is beautifully printed, of convenient size for use, and of admirable adaptation to the service of those whose Hebrew has become a dim reminiscence." — *North American Review.*

Hebrew Psalter. ספר תהלים. Liber Psalmorum. Text according to Hahn. 32mo. Morocco. pp. 177. $1.00

This is the smallest pocket edition, and is altogether the most convenient Hebrew Psalter ever published in this country. It is printed in very clear type.

"To those who read Hebrew this little volume will be a perfect diamond. We have seen nothing for many a day which has pleased our fancy more. The paper is excellent, the printing remarkably clear and distinct, and the general appearance of the *booklet* like a gem of the first water — which it is." — *Christian Secretary.*

H

Lightfoot. **St. Paul's Epistle to the Galatians.** A Revised Text, with Introduction, Notes, and Dissertations. By J. B. LIGHT-FOOT, D.D., Hulsean Professor of Divinity, and Fellow of Trinity College, Cambridge. 8vo. pp. 402. Uniform in style with Ellicott Henderson and Murphy. $3.00

" This work aims to be, and in some respects is, more complete than any other treatise upon the Epistle in the English language. Great labor and learning are expended upon collateral discussions. Indeed, the commentary on the text forms the smaller part of the volume, invested as it is with elaborate dissertations and detached notes, before and after and between.

" The commentary is learned without display. It bears marks throughout of wide and scholarly research held in strict subordination to the purpose of exposition. All theories except those which *deserve* a consideration are left out of the account. Perhaps the collateral dissertations might have been similarly compressed. It is independent. Few commentaries bear more clearly the tokens of freedom from constraint. The author apparently does not swerve from his course either to agree with or differ from any other writer. He decides for himself upon the text, after a revision by Westcott for his use. . . . . And this leads us to say that it is largely marked by a manly insight. He reaches his results less by that process of exclusion which so characterizes Ellicott, and more by a direct apprehension ; and he often holds them, perhaps, with more of an instinctive certainty than Alford. . . . . It is spiritual and evangelical." — *Congregational Review.*

" For a scholar's use Dr. Lightfoot's Commentary is invaluable. He and Bishop Ellicott worthily supplement each other. The Revised Text is one of the best recent contributions to a complete text to the Greek New Testament, and the criticisms on the text are concise and to the point," etc. — *Am. Presbyterian Review.*

" Taken as a whole, we venture to say that this is the most complete and exhaustive commentary on the Epistle to the Galatians that has yet appeared, Ellicott's not excepted." — *Christian Intelligencer.*

Reubelt. **The Scripture Doctrine of the Person of Christ.** By J. A. REUBELT, D.D., Professor in Indiana University, Bloomington, Ind., based on the German of W. F. Gess. 12mo. pp. 456. Cloth, $2.00

" As a whole, this treatise may be briefly characterized as an earnest and able effort to present the true and consistent doctrine of the Scriptures respecting the person of Christ, and to reconcile the varying confessional statements and views of different denominations, by carefully comparing them with the language of the Scriptures themselves. The investigation is conducted in a devout, candid and truth-loving spirit, combined with accurate scholarship and thorough study of the subject." — *Lutheran Observer.*

" The translator has executed his task with admirable skill. While preserving the integrity of the original as to its line of thought and argument, he has clothed it in excellent English." — *Christian Intelligencer.*

" Those who hold the doctrine of eternal generation will here find a valuable aid in divesting their views of its customary crudeness, and sublimating, as far as may be, the inherent contradiction that lies in the two words. We are content with that view of the phrase, "only-begotten Son," which regards it as setting forth by a human relationship (as usual) everywhere significant, but especially so to a Jew, the unity of nature, possession, purpose, interest, and sympathy which characterize the Father and the Son." — *Congregational Review.*

" Though the style of thought is peculiar, and though the opinions are often new, and sometimes such as may not command immediate assent, or even command assent at all, yet there is an awakening power in the book, and the drift of it is right." — *Congregationalist.*

WARREN F. DRAPER, Publisher,
34
Andover, Mass.

Winer. *A Grammar of the Idiom of the New Testament:* prepared as a Solid Basis for the Interpretation of the New Testament. By DR. GEORGE BENEDICT WINER. Seventh edition, enlarged and improved. By DR. GOTTLIEB LÜNEMANN, Professor of Theology at the University of Göttingen. Revised and Authorized Translation. 8vo. pp. 744.

Cloth, $5.00 ; sheep, $6.00 ; half goat, $6.75

"After his death a seventh edition of his Grammar was published in 1866, under the editorial care of Dr. Lünemann. This editor incorporated into this edition the numerous manuscript notes which Winer had prepared for it. ' Without altering the general distribution of matter as it appeared in the sixth edition, he [Winer] constantly improved the book in details, by additions of greater or less extent in more than three hundred and forty places, by erasures and reconstructions, by the multiplication of parallel passages from biblical and from profane literature, by a more precise definition of thoughts and expressions,' etc. Professor Lünemann has added to the seventh edition not only these improvements, but also improvements of his own ; and has thus made the seventh edition more full, as well as more accurate, than either of the preceding.

" The first edition of Winer's Grammar was translated into English by Professors Stuart and Robinson in 1825 ; the fourth edition by Professors Agnew and Ebbeke in 1839 ; the sixth edition, translated by Professor Masson, was published at Edinburgh, and his translation of the sixth is the basis of Professor Thayer's translation of the seventh [Lünemann's] edition. Professor Thayer, however, has introduced numerous and important corrections of Masson's translation, and has made the present edition of the Grammar decidedly superior to any of the preceding translations. He has made it especially convenient for the uses of an English student, by noting on the outer margin of the pages the paging of the sixth and seventh German editions, and also of Professor Masson's translation. Thus the reader of a commentary which refers to the pages of either of those volumes, may easily find the reference by consulting the margin of this volume. Great care has also been bestowed on the indexes of the present volume, which are now very accurate and complete. One of the indexes, that of passages in the New Testament explained or cited occupies sixty pages, and notes distinctively not only the texts which are merely cited, but also those which are commented upon. For this, much credit is due to Professor G. W. Warren, of the Baptist Theological Seminary in Chicago. The three indexes fill eighty-five pages, and largely augment the value and richness of the volume. The typographical execution of the book also deserves praise ; so far as we have examined it, we have been surprised at its correctness in places where the types are apt to err." — *Bibliotheca Sacra.*

" The work of the American editor is done in a thorough and scholarly manner." — *Congregational Quarterly.*

" While nothing has been done by either the American or German editor to alter the character and plan of the work as Winer left it after the labor of a life, nothing has been left undone to correct and complete it, and provide for its more extended usefulness." — *Princeton Review.*

" The whole appearance of the work as it now stands indicates a careful and thorough scholarship. A critical comparison of several pages with the original confirms the impression made by a general examination of the book. In its present form, this translation may now be recommended as worthy of a place in the library of every minister who desires to study the New Testament with the aid of the best critical helps." — *Theological Eclectic.*

" Great pains also have been taken to secure typographical accuracy, an extremely difficult thing in a work of this kind. We rejoice that so invaluable a work has thus been made as nearly perfect as we can hope ever to have it. It is a work that can hardly fail to facilitate and increase the reverent and accurate study of the Word of God." — *American Presbyterian Review.*

www.ingramcontent.com/pod-product-compliance
Lightning Source LLC
Chambersburg PA
CBHW020228090426
42735CB00010B/1624